Living the Difference

Living the Difference

**an enlightening story revealed for
people of all ages straight or gay**

J. C. Knudson

Espresso House Publishing & Distribution

LIVING THE DIFFERENCE
an enlightening story revealed for people of all ages straight or gay

Cover Photo © 2010 JupiterImages Corporation. All rights reserved - used with permission.

Illustrations done by Robert Wood, rwood@masterworkmurals.com

Espresso House Publishing & Distribution, LLC
7532 W. Fordson Dr.
Oklahoma City, Oklahoma 73127

PB ISBN: 978-0-578-06271-6

Library of Congress Control Number: 2010931967

PRINTED IN THE UNITED STATES OF AMERICA

This book is dedicated to my wonderful parents, my two grown sons, and the love of my life for over seventeen years. I was blessed with the opportunity to care for each of my parents during their last few years of life on this earth; while that experience wasn't always a positive one as you'll see, it's one I'd do over and over again. I'm also blessed with being the father of two fantastic and tremendously fine young men; my life would be ever so different, in a negative way, if they weren't a part of it. Last and by no means least is my significant other, words don't do justice nor could relay the positive impact he's had and continues to have on my existence here on earth. I love you all dearly!

I'd like to give special mention to my ex-wife; without her understanding, my coming out would've been extremely more difficult than it was. She's also a fantastic mother to our two sons and I thank her dearly for that. She'll always have a special place in my heart! My brother also deserves special mention as without the love and support of his entire family throughout the many tough times in my life, making it through those tough times would've been more grueling than it was. The last special mention includes every one of my pets throughout the years; they were always at my side no matter what, especially my dog Felix, who to this day is always at my side.

Table of Contents

Preface i
About The Author v
1: Early Awareness 1
2: New Journey, New Places...13
3: Next Few Corners..29
4: Early Career 47
5: What Next...67
6: Coming Out..79
7: Gay Dating..91
8: Settling Into The Right Relationship 107
9: Admitting A Wrong Decision, Going Forward 129
10: Position Of Persecution, Life Went On 135
11: Yet Another Battle.. 161
12: Proceeding Ahead With Surgery And Family 175
13: Life's Journey Saddens 191
14: Finding The Light Again And Continuing On 207
15: The Beginning Of Something New 219

Preface

Acquired behavior or genetic makeup, what do you believe? After personally researching major medical and theological studies on the issue, as well as beliefs by various laymen and laywomen, I've always come back to and relied on my own experiences and inner feelings as to the origin of my own homosexuality. This book isn't intended to convince readers of any one belief over another, nor provide the details of the various beliefs; the sole purpose is to tell my own personal story from the bottom of my heart and allow readers to reach their own conclusions once that additional knowledge has been gained.

I'm a fifty five year old divorced gay father of two with many colorful and certain not so colorful experiences throughout my life I'd like to share with everyone. I feel by sharing my experiences I might just make a difference; not only in the life of someone who believes they may be homosexual, but also in the life of someone attempting to understand and be supportive of a friend or loved one who has recently come out, as well as anyone with just a slight curiosity as to what it's like being homosexual. I trust and believe I will assist one in finding solace, inner piece, and a complete understanding of themselves and others upon reading this book, as well as being thoroughly entertained in the process. Additionally, certain assurances many times so hard to come by in this not so understanding world we live in, if gained, will be mere icing on the cake.

The journey through the various chapters of my life you're about to begin will continue in upcoming sequels, depicting certain individual chapters or subject matters in this book in books of their own, with any and all questions answered in full living color as each sequel delves deeper into all the enticing details.

Please sit back and relax through an excitedly tense, informative, orgasmic, and at times painful journey of truth, lies, love, hate, fun, drudgery, ridicule, rape, bribery, legal hassles, anxiety, depression, suicide attempts, and cancer. The trials and tribulations I've endured have made me a stronger individual; experiencing the corresponding highs, lows, successes, and failures have renewed my faith in God that everyone of us are on this earth for a purpose and a part of my purpose in life is to help and enlighten others.

If by reference or non-reference I've offended anyone in telling my story, I sincerely apologize and trust you know in your heart that wasn't my intent. Certain details of various events, including certain events themselves throughout this book, have been altered to protect the innocent and any similarities to the actual details or events are merely coincidental.

About The Author

Joseph C. Knudson (J.C.) was born December 10, 1954, in Watertown, South Dakota and resided in Florence, South Dakota, a small rural town twenty miles away. He's the youngest of four children born to Richard K. and Madeline M. Trautner Knudson and was named after the local parish priest.

In 1967 the Knudson family relocated to Guymon, Oklahoma, were J.C. graduated from Guymon High School in 1973 with honors.

J.C. married his high school sweetheart in 1974. The marriage lasted several years; before being divorced, he and his wife adopted two loving boys.

In 1977 J.C. graduated from Panhandle State University in Goodwell, Oklahoma, with numerous honors and achievements. He received a *Bachelor of Science in Accounting and Business Administration.*

Upon graduation from college, J.C. and his wife moved to Oklahoma City, Oklahoma, where both still reside today in separate households.

J.C. met his significant other in 1992; they've been together ever since and have continually provided a loving, nurturing environment for each of their sons.

In 1995 J.C. assisted in the design, manufacture, and distribution of the *Oklahoma City Bombing Memorial Pin*, helping to raise money for the victims and families of the April 19, 1995 bombing of the *Alfred P. Murrah Federal Building* in Oklahoma City.

In 1996 J.C. and his significant other, through their own company IMC, designed the *Oklahoma City Bombing Anniversary Bible Necklace*; distribution of the necklace on the one year anniversary of the Oklahoma City bombing continued the fundraising efforts.

J.C. received a letter dated April 27, 1996 from then Governor of Oklahoma, Frank Keating, thanking him for the support, through his fundraising efforts, for the victims and families of the Oklahoma City bombing and informing him one of the bible necklaces would be included with the memorial exhibit in the *Blue Room* of the state capital building. Another letter dated June 4, 1996 was received from then President of the United States, Bill Clinton, expressing his and Hillary's appreciation for J.C.'s fundraising efforts.

In efforts to expand his own business, a brief temporary move was made to Colorado, with a permanent move back to Oklahoma City in 1997.

The next several years provided numerous challenges in many dire and diverse situations for J.C.; when all said and done, the challenges made him a stronger individual with a better knowledge and understanding of what motivates people and their corresponding behavior toward others. Many of these situations are covered in the contents of this book.

J.C. has written numerous pieces of poetry with publication of several of his pieces in hardcover national publications on three separate occasions.

1

Early Awareness

My sense of awareness as to my sexual preferences began early on in life. While most children at the age of five and younger were fully content playing with toys, watching cartoons, and all the other fun things to do at preschool, in addition to those, I was always mesmerized when I saw a handsome man. That fixation on men would at times occur out of nowhere, seeing a man in a television commercial, taking lunch out to the hired hands on the farm, watching older male students play basketball at the high school games, and many other remembrances.

One such remembrance being the family outings we'd take to Medicine Lake. Medicine Lake was a small salt water lake out in the sticks. From my earliest recollection of existence, the family would escape to the lake during many of the dreadful hot humid days of summer. It was the place to be for summer fun, relaxation, and a dip in the cool water. People were everywhere in the water, on the giant floating diving platform, and stretched out on beach blankets along the sandy shores of the lake. It seemed like paradise to me. Not only did I enjoy all the fun, but being the cute little kid I was, enjoyed all the attention the older guys would give me in trying to show off and impress the girls by teaching me to swim, taking me out to the deep water on their shoulders, and taking me to the concession stand buying me candy and pop. At the time, I remember it giving me a warm inner feeling being around the older guys, more than just the attention I was getting.

CHILDHOOD FUN AT THE LAKE

LIVING THE DIFFERENCE

I hadn't an idea why those feelings would come over me. It wasn't the absence of male role models at home because I had my dad and older brother ten years my senior. We were a fairly close knit family and before you begin to wonder, to my recollection, there was no molestation of any kind within the family or elsewhere. Of course, just being a preschooler, I imagined all boys had those feelings when it came to seeing and being around a man, that it was a normal part of growing up. So I was content for the time thinking it was normal, even though none of my friends ever mentioned anything of that nature.

I remember one evening in particular my older sister brought her date home for my parents to meet; he'd picked her up after drama practice at school and they were going out for the evening. He was quite the looker and smelled good to boot. Everyone sat in the living room, with me in the middle of everything. When my sister introduced him to me he shook my hand and immediately I was mesmerized. As they were about to leave she asked me if I'd like to go get something to eat with them. I couldn't believe my ears and immediately replied yes. I already had my pajamas on so I ran upstairs to change. We went to the Dairy Queen drive in and I ordered my favorite, a foot long and a banana milkshake. After we finished eating they dropped me off at home and continued on with their date. He was all I could think about that evening.

As time went on and I was further along in grade school the feelings were still there. Whenever I'd see a man and become fixated on him, I'd look around at my friends trying to see if they were taking a special interest in the same man, but it was hard to tell. I started taking the late school bus home so I could join after school activities at the gym because there were always older male students shooting hoops and I enjoyed being around looking at them. I especially looked forward to when my mother would get her new department store catalogs in the mail, whenever I was the only one around, I'd flip through the catalogs to the male underwear section and look at the men; the summer catalogs were especially exciting to get as they had a swimsuit section and I could see a little more of the men without having to go to Medicine Lake.

I finally began to wonder if I was different than other young boys. Especially when I'd hear some of my friends talk about finding their dad's girlie magazines somewhere around the house and enjoyed looking at them. At that point, it became a little more difficult to deal with the feelings. Did I pretend I didn't have those feelings and try to ignore them? Should I've gone along with the gang looking at the girlie magazines whenever they'd sneak them out; I remember saying to myself, "What should I do?" Well, I pretended and I lied. I pretended I liked looking at magazines with pictures of naked women. I'd even make over the pictures more than the other kids, thinking if I was going to lie I might as well do it up right and sound convincing; I was petrified they'd find out I was different and wouldn't like me or hang around with me anymore.

I kind of wondered if just maybe I tried hard enough to enjoy the naked pictures I might grow to enjoy looking at girls more than I did guys.

Time went on; I continued trying to ignore my true feelings and even tried to think of ways to change myself so I could be like the other guys. I quit looking through the department store catalogs and tried to distance myself from being around men other than my dad, brother, and grade school friends. I also stopped going to high school basketball games. While I didn't want to, I even stopped staying after school and going to the gym as well; I'd catch the early bus and go directly home after school to watch afternoon cartoons. I was hoping the feelings would just go away. At one point, I remember praying to God that I'd start liking girls more than guys; I grew up Catholic and even considered talking to my priest in the confessional about my infatuation, but was afraid of what he'd say. I knew he was bound to secrecy and couldn't discuss anything we talked about with anyone, but I was still scared he might tell my parents.

By that time my father had stopped farming and sold the farm to a neighboring farmer. We'd already moved in town and at least that kept me from running into any hired hands.

I continually tried other methods of stopping the infatuation because I was determined to be like the other guys. It's hard at times for me to even remember how much pressure I put myself under to change. I was always popular in school so it was very important for that change to take place and not let anyone know of my inner feelings I so desperately wanted to get rid of.

A new school year started, I was elected prince of the grade school homecoming assembly and had to walk up on stage with the princess. As we were on stage the guys were yelling, "Kiss her, come on J.C. plant one on her." I was trembling and didn't know what to do, before I realized what I was doing, I leaned over planting a big one right on her lips. I was cheered by everyone at the assembly, but got in trouble by our principal and had to stay after school in detention. I was still glad I did it because I knew everyone would think I liked girls and would never know about those other inner feelings.

As it turned out the princess liked the kiss and we kind of started to hang out together at recess, lunch, and after school. I was ok with that as I was kind of a hero and thought possibly I might be changing. We even exchanged Christmas gifts that year; however, after we came back from the holiday break, I just didn't have the desire to continue hanging around her, even though she still wanted everyone to believe we were seeing each other. One day after school she cornered me outside the classroom and surprised me by planting her own big one right on my lips; I have to tell you it grossed me out. I tried hard to avoid her the remainder of the school year as I just couldn't bring myself to any more of those big ones, at least until I figured out if I was supposed to enjoy them, just not yet to that point in my life, therefore not needing to change, or if I actually was different and would never enjoy them unless I could change.

The school year ended and summer began; I was still determined to figure things out and change, if necessary, before school started back in the fall. I wanted more than anything to be normal.

Early that summer a new family moved in a few blocks down the street from our house. As I was riding my bike past their house one day a kid who looked to be my age asked if I wanted to play croquet; I did and we had a great time playing. We became friends and hung out together that entire summer.

Something was different with my new friend and I thought just maybe he may have that same fixation with men I was trying to get over. I couldn't pinpoint what made me feel that way, guess I just had a hunch. He was the only one I ever had that hunch about at that age, which I now realize wasn't that big of a deal as chances were slim there'd be any others; I grew up in a very small rural community and our total grade school population, grades one through six, was less than one hundred students total, boys and girls.

Another school year began and in a few weeks the school track team I was a member of was preparing for a meet at another school about twenty miles away. My new friend asked if I wanted to spend the night before the meet at his house and we could walk together in the morning to the activity bus taking us. My mom was fine with that. I was excited and on the day before the meet took a suitcase packed with what I needed to school so I could go directly home with him after school. We had a fun evening, his mother made home made pizza and we had ice cream before we went to bed. We talked about the upcoming meet while we were in bed and just as I was about to fall asleep, I felt his hand touch my crotch. Wow, I was surprised and confused; let's just say the sheets rose a little.

I didn't know what to say to him the next day at the meet or if I should even say anything. The day went about as one would expect; we had fun, laughed a lot, won some events, ate hotdogs, and drank a lot of pop. Nothing ever came up about the evening before. I had some thinking to do. I was trying so hard to be normal, but I knew what happened that evening was probably not normal. I decided not to concentrate on it and just try to have fun as a kid.

We remained friends, but I was scared to bring him into my group of school friends; the town being small and part of the rural community, many of my school friends lived in the country on farms, the only time we really hung out was during the school year. I worried he'd tell the other guys about that evening. It turned out I was worrying for nothing as the other guys didn't like him because they thought he was a sissy, so now I had to decide if I wanted to hang with him or the other guys. I decided to hang with the other guys at school.

LIVING THE DIFFERENCE

It kind of relieved me the others thought he was a sissy because that told me they didn't have that same thought about me. It was really strange though because on weekends and holiday breaks that school year, I'd still hang with him and he never questioned why I didn't at school. Just maybe he was different; since nothing ever came up about that evening before the track meet, he probably thought I was normal and he should leave well enough alone. Gosh, what a confusing time in my life; different, same, normal, not normal, it's a miracle I made it through grade school in one piece.

Speaking of one piece, a bombshell was dropped on our family by my dad right before that school year ended and I felt my life was about to scatter in a million pieces. He came home from work one evening and told all of us the plant he worked at was closing their doors within a short time; he was being transferred to a new facility that was a sixteen hour drive away and in another state. I shouted out, "Are all of us going?" I knew better! My brother had been out of the house since college days, while my older sister was about to move after her upcoming marriage at the time, and my eighty year old grandma, my only living grandparent, was in ill health not wanting to make such a move; that only left me and my other sister.

I didn't need that news dropped on me. My own hands were full figuring myself out and being a regular kid trying to enjoy my childhood. Now I'd be moving to a new state, starting a new school, living in a new neighborhood, and meeting new friends. What did all of this mean to me? It meant starting all over trying to fit in as a normal guy in new surroundings with new people, while at the same time continuing to deal with the fact I was, in all likelihood, different than most guys my age and was trying desperately to change.

That was my first experience with depression. My mom was worried about me and assumed the depression was just mere anxiety over the upcoming move. She'd talk with me trying to ease my fears and wanted me to look at the move as a new adventure full of fun and excitement, along with a certain amount of mystery involved. She had no idea there was a tremendous amount of mystery involved. I wanted to tell my mom everything, but I just couldn't.

Before I knew it, it was the day the semi-truck came to load up our belongings and I had a couple hours to say my goodbyes. It was in the middle of summer and many of my friends were away on vacation, summer camp, or visiting relatives. I did get to say goodbye to a few, but couldn't find the one I really wanted to say goodbye to. I was really sad because I wanted to apologize to him for the way I treated him at times during the school year when the other guys were around; I basically ignored him at those times. I wasn't proud of myself for the way I acted and really wanted him to know. He knew we were moving and just maybe didn't want to say goodbye. I was just hoping to play a farewell game of croquet with him and a part of me really wanted to tell him about myself before I moved since he was the only other guy I knew who may have been different like I was. I was about to move sixteen hours away so there would've been no damaging repercussions in telling him.

I got back to the house and went in the back door; dad told me we were about ready to pull out and grandma was out front in her car waiting to say goodbye to me. I ran out front to see grandma and say goodbye, we both began to cry. It was very hard to leave her as close as we were to each other; at that time, she was the only other person in my life I would've considered confiding in. The semi-truck had already pulled out and the cars were loaded ready to go. My mom, dad, and sister rode in the family car and I rode with my brother in his car as he'd taken a vacation from his job out of state to help us move.

We had a sixteen hour trip ahead of us and I was embarking on a new chapter in my life.

2

New Journey, New Places

Wow, a sixteen hour trip ahead and I was alone in the car with my brother. What would I talk to him about for so long? Was he going to realize I was different? Since my brother was ten years older we really hadn't spent that much time together. When I was eight, he was graduating from high school and ready to go off to business school. He didn't come home that often from business school because he worked whenever he wasn't in class.

There I was, nervous as all get out and it was just my brother. I wanted him to think I was cool and normal. One of the first things out of my mouth was, "Did you know I had a girlfriend once?" What a stupid thing to say. He asked me if I was going to miss her and I said, without even giving it a thought, "Nope!" He said I'd probably meet some nice southern girls in Oklahoma when I began junior high the next school year.

LIVING THE DIFFERENCE

He had a new girlfriend and they both worked together so I asked about her. I'm glad I did because that was all he could talk about for the next hour or so and that got me off the hook by helping time pass quickly. All I could think of at the time was that I wished I could be like my brother.

Before I knew it the hours passed quickly. We were going though one town after another and the scenery was all new to me. I was actually beginning to have fun. For the first time since I was told we'd be moving, I honestly thought the move might be good for me; boy was my mom going to be glad when I told her.

The town we were moving to was about ten times larger than where we were coming from; however, that's not saying much. At least the new place had a bowling alley and a movie screen; I'd never bowled and only been to a couple drive in movies. The closer we got to our new home, the more excited I became; I couldn't wait to check everything out. That was the first time in a long time however different I may have been didn't seem to matter at that point.

We'd been trailing the family car most the trip as my brother had the newer car; in case the family car broke down, we'd come upon it and be able to help. We finally arrived and pulled up to the new family home, it was brand new; mom and dad had been down a month prior and purchased it from the builder. After we settled in a bit that day, my brother hit me with a big surprise. In a couple days he was going on down to Mexico for a little vacation and wanted me to go with him. I was so excited I began to cry, as never before in my life did I have so many good things go on all at once that made me feel so happy and free.

Before we left for Mexico, I met some kids around my age on the block we'd just moved to. I didn't have time to get to know them as I was extremely busy getting ready for the trip. It was just as well, I didn't have to worry about what they thought of me and would have all kinds of exciting things to tell them when I returned from the trip. What a great way to break the ice with new friends.

My brother and I left before dawn the next morning, boy was I excited. To be going to another country was like a dream come true. I thought if this could happen so could a change in my feelings. I even began to wonder if I dare talk to my brother and possibly ask if he ever had any type of fixation on men growing up.

We drove for a couple hours and stopped for breakfast; while we were waiting on our food he called his girlfriend from the payphone inside. I thought he'd never come back to the table. The waitress brought our food so I went over to the payphone to tell my brother and he said he'd be right there. A few minutes passed and still no brother. I went ahead and ate my food as I was starved, finally he came back to scarf down his. It seemed like every couple hours we'd stop for something; finally I realized it was only an excuse for him to use a payphone and call his girlfriend. I didn't really know what love was at the time other than the love I had for my parents, but I began to realize there was another type of love, the love my brother obviously had for his girlfriend, a love I wondered if I could ever have with a girl.

In a few more hours we arrived at *Carlsbad Caverns* in New Mexico. We took a tour of the caverns and ate in the restaurant at the bottom. Again, he had to make that special telephone call; I realized there was no need to talk to him about me as how could he ever have had any type of fixation on men as fixated as he was with his girlfriend. Right after the caverns, we drove just a short while before deciding to find a motel and stop for the night. We were both extremely tired and worn out; I'm sure he was more worn out from talking on the telephone than anything else.

The next morning we got up early and drove on down to El Paso, Texas, just across the border from Juarez, Mexico. We parked the car and walked across the border to begin our sightseeing. We went to the old market, ate some authentic Mexican food, and then took a cab to the bullfighting arena. There wasn't another bullfight scheduled for a few hours and my brother didn't want to wait so we just walked around the bullpens looking at the bulls. There was a gift shop close by, he wanted to go inside and look around; that really didn't interest me so I just walked around the arena. As I was walking around I came upon another bullpen, but the bull wasn't alone in that one, there were also two guys inside that appeared to be making out. I stood there a moment and watched, sure enough they were. Again, one of those special warm inner feelings came over me and it felt great. I turned around and my brother was walking up behind me so I walked extremely fast toward him yelling, "I have to go to the bathroom real bad." I really didn't, I just wanted to get him away from that bullpen so he wouldn't see what I saw. We both went to the bathroom and then left the arena.

For some reason my brother was ready to cross back to El Paso and look around there. I thought we'd spend more time in Mexico, but thinking back he probably couldn't call his girlfriend from another country and wanted to get back to Texas so he could. We didn't stay long in El Paso either, after just a couple hours he wanted to head back to Oklahoma. Immediately, I wondered if he saw what I saw at the arena; I began to worry he did and was wondering about me.

BULLSEYE VIEW OF TWO GUYS MAKING OUT

NEW JOURNEY, NEW PLACES

As we began our drive back he said he wanted to make a little detour. He wanted to stop at *White Sands National Park* and get a little of the white sand to take back with him. I hadn't heard of the place and got a little excited. We arrived and there were white sand dunes as far as the eye could see. We got out of the car and walked around. While I was writing my name in the sand I noticed he was doing the same, except he was also writing another name, yes his girlfriends.

We didn't talk much on the way back. I was continually thinking about what I saw at the arena, mulling it over in my mind, while I assumed he was thinking about his girlfriend and couldn't wait to get back to her. At least I was hoping that's what his mind was occupied with and not seeing what I saw.

We finally arrived and pulled in the driveway in the wee hours of the morning. After waking up our parents and unloading my things, my brother decided not to unload his; he immediately got back on the road so he could get home himself. I then realized all he had on his mind was getting back to his girlfriend.

When I finally got up later that day I helped my mom unpack the rest of our belongings that were still in boxes from the move. We worked the rest of the day until dad got home from work. We went out to eat that evening as mom was tired from all the unpacking and when we got home all of us went to bed early. I remember I couldn't sleep that night because all I could think about were those two guys making out in the bullpen; I wondered what it was like. I finally drifted off to sleep and woke up early the next morning.

That next day I had to pre-enroll in junior high because school was to begin in a couple weeks. One of the kids I met before I went to Mexico lived next door and we were in the same grade; his mother drove us to the school to pre-enroll. After enrolling, we walked around the junior high school and it was really going to be different for me. Every class was in a different room and some even in different buildings. I was somewhat intimidated, but was determined I'd be able to handle it.

The rest of the day I spent with my new friend, we just goofed off and messed around some. We shot at targets with his bow and arrow and at tin cans with my BB gun. He seemed like a pretty cool guy. He had a friend who had a couple horses so he took me over to meet him and see the horses. I really got around that day and met a lot of new people. I never got around to telling anyone about my trip to Mexico; that was ok with me because the most memorable part of that trip was seeing the two guys make out and I wasn't about to tell anyone about that.

Summer vacation was over and it was time to start junior high school. I was excited, yet a little apprehensive. The first day rolled around and it wasn't good. I was spat on and teased some; naturally, I thought it was because of my infatuation with men and everyone could tell, even though I made it a point not to look at any guy more than just a passing glance.

It was all totally different for me; it wasn't young kids from grade school anymore, it was older more mature guys I'd be going to school with. It wasn't only that, I'd grown too and matured in many ways; I definitely realized my infatuation was growing and maturing along with me.

I didn't say anything to anyone about that first day, even my parents. Many other families moved to Oklahoma that same summer, all from South Dakota where I came from. They were relocated for the same reason my family was, transferred from a plant closing back home to a new facility in Oklahoma. It eventually came to be known other kids from South Dakota were also teased, even the girls. Supposedly we had an unusual accent when we spoke. However, none of the other kids from South Dakota ever admitted to having been spat on; appears that was exclusive to me. I prayed it was an isolated instance and nothing more.

There was nothing easy about that first year in junior high other than the studies; I always excelled in school and that didn't change with the new school. To this day I don't believe anyone at that point realized I was different other than for my accent. It was just difficult fitting in and feeling comfortable in my new surroundings that first year.

Summer arrived and I started delivering newspapers to earn spending money. I also mowed and took care of yards, as well as other odd jobs that summer. I met a lot of new kids, some becoming close friends and some not so close. One friend in particular, who I wasn't that close to, was always asking if I'd shot my wad yet, I didn't know what that meant so I always said no. One day he said he couldn't shoot his yet and wanted to help me try to shoot mine, again I said no.

Later in the summer I needed to train someone as a substitute carrier for my newspaper route because I was going to be gone a few days; guess what, the only person I found willing was the kid who hadn't shot his wad. He went with me a few days to become familiar with my route. A couple evenings before I was to be gone, he asked to spend the night at my house so he could ask questions and be sure he knew everything about the route. By the next morning not only did we get all his questions answered, but we also got my wad shot; I had no idea what he was doing or what was going on, he did all the work and shot mine for me. What a summer to remember! There was definitely something different about that evening compared to earlier in grade school when a friend touched my crotch in bed. I didn't get the feeling my new friend had an infatuation with men, only a curiosity with puberty.

Eighth grade was definitely a better year for me. I started to lose my accent and picked up some Oklahoma slang such as *ya all*; I didn't even get spat on. I made several friends that year and felt considerably more comfortable with my new surroundings; well, a least most of them. I had a difficult time with PE class; it wasn't the class itself, it was afterward in the shower. We had to take a shower after class and there was just one large communal shower. Looking at the other guys didn't bother me, I rather enjoyed it immensely; the problem was keeping a certain body part under control. I used a lot of deodorant that school year and skipped many showers. If I had any previous doubts about my sexual preferences, most of them were erased that school year.

I worked the majority of the time the next summer because I was saving money to buy my own car when I turned sixteen; I was also buying most of my own clothes by that time. I was able to work in a trip back to South Dakota to visit friends and relatives; I caught a ride with another family previously from South Dakota. I had a great time seeing everyone and even ran into my croquet buddy. We really got reacquainted and had a fun time in the process; my earlier hunch was right on. I stayed a couple weeks and ended up taking a bus back to Oklahoma.

The bus ride back to Oklahoma was quite an experience. Other than a school bus, I'd never been on a commercial travel bus. The trip was extremely long, exhausting, and very hot; they didn't have air conditioners in travel buses at that time or at least that one didn't. The bus did have a bathroom, but it was much smaller than the old toilet outhouse back when I lived on a farm. We'd stop quite frequently at bus stations along the way both to drop off and pick up passengers. While we were stopped, if it was close to a mealtime, we were expected to eat and hurry back on the bus.

The only thing that made the trip bearable was a passenger who boarded the bus in Sioux Falls; he was on his way to college in Texas. He sat next to me the remainder of the trip, he was very nice. We were both bored out of our minds so we thought of games we could play to pass the time away. We had loads of fun. It wasn't a sleeper bus so it was very difficult trying to catch any sleep; the seats reclined a little and the armrests were adjustable. The first night I couldn't sleep at all, he snored all night long; I'd nudge him at times thinking that'd make him stop. One of my nudges finally woke him up and he felt bad about keeping me awake. He told me he'd stay awake; he wanted me to spread out and try to get some sleep. He said to lean over against him if that'd give me more room to spread out. I did and I slept like a baby. When I woke up, I was leaning way over against him; he was asleep with his head back on the seat and his arm spread out around me. I couldn't help the feeling that came over me, it felt real good being so close to him and I didn't want him to wake up.

Ninth grade rolled around and brought a year of uncertainty for me. Classes were great; it was the year of the *queer* that messed things up. A new student arrived; he was very flamboyant and hung around girls. Most the guys teased him and called him a *queer*. I didn't know what to think. He was definitely different, but I didn't consider him different like I considered myself different. I hadn't been around anyone as girlish as he was. I even thought there was hope for me that my fixation on men could eventually change because I was nothing like him. Maybe I was just going through a phase in my life, a long phase. I definitely didn't associate with him. I even started dating a girl to see if it'd be different since I'd grown and matured. Don't get me wrong, I still had that fixation on men, I just wanted to experiment some with dating a girl.

One day after classes, some of the guys were talking about a big fight that was about to take place in an alley behind the school. Everyone was headed that way so I followed. Sure enough when we arrived, there were two guys fighting it out. I couldn't tell who they were at first, but it didn't take long to realize it was the new student and one of the football players. The fight didn't last very long and when it was over, it was the football player on the ground with a cut lip and bloody nose, the new student walked away with torn trousers and dirty clothes. I thought to myself right on! The joy of seeing that didn't last long because later in the week a group of football players beat the heck out of the new student on his way home from school.

I continued to date the same girl for the remainder of the school year. Nothing exciting happened. We'd kiss, make out, went to a couple games, and even went to a couple movies, but nothing ever got my juices flowing. Was it her, was it me; I just didn't know. Before the school year ended I told her it just wasn't working for me and it ended.

Summer began and I got a new job. I went to work for a janitorial cleaning service. It was the only cleaning service in town and we stayed extremely busy. Most of the work was after five in the evening and many nights we'd work till two or three in the morning. Weekends were packed and we worked most of both days. Many times the owner of the service would drop me off and I'd clean certain businesses alone; when I finished early and he wasn't due back I'd have time to goof off, which wasn't always a good thing. One evening in particular I was finished and got bored so I went through a desk drawer in one of the offices. I found a stack of dirty magazines and started flipping through them. I got excited and aroused with a picture of a man and woman getting it on; before I knew it someone opened the door, walked in the office, and caught me with my pants down. It wasn't my boss it was someone coming back after hours to get caught up on some work. I was scared to death he'd tell my boss and I'd get fired. He was a very nice guy and said it wasn't anything he probably didn't do when he was my age.

With all the work I slept whenever I'd find the time. I made a lot of money that summer, but my social life sucked. It was just as well because I was so darn confused about my feelings, fixations, and infatuations that I wouldn't have known what to do anyway.

I went through a mild depression just before summer

ended; I was getting ready to begin high school in a few weeks not knowing who I really was. I went to the public library one day before work to find anything it might have on homosexuality. I was afraid to ask the librarian so I looked on my own. Remember it was 1970, you'd think a public library would have books on any subject matter at that time; obviously not. At least I couldn't locate any; maybe it was because it was a small town library or the fact Oklahoma was in the Bible belt. We didn't have the internet back then, nor did we have the large chains of bookstores like we do now. I was out of luck on finding any material on the subject at that time.

Another corner of my life was upon me and I was proceeding ahead with caution!

3

Next Few Corners

There I was taking the next corner and I wasn't even six-teen yet. It seemed to me I'd been around too many dan-gerously new and sharp corners for my age. At times, I wondered if I was maturing too quick and needed to slow down, but how could one slow down at that age with so much mystery and uncertainty.

My sophomore year started out great with new teach-ers, new students, new friends, new surroundings, and the excitement of turning sixteen in a few months. Not that turning sixteen would automatically change my feelings or make everything perfect; the anticipation of it at least occupied some of my thought process at the time and the fact of actually obtaining a driving license was excitement in itself.

I enrolled in the required driving education class that year even though my dad previously taught me how to drive; it was a requirement in obtaining an Oklahoma driving license. The class instructor was a jerk; he was also a coach who'd slap you up the side of your head if you did anything he thought was stupid. Well, a few weeks into the class I did something stupid, I fell outside the classroom and broke my leg. It was a bad break in a couple different places and I ended up being transferred to a specialty hospital in a much larger city. Due to the required therapy the doctor ordered, I was there over a week and came out wearing a cast from my thigh all the way down to my toes, with crutches a part of the standard issue. One of the first thoughts I had was if the driving instructor would let me back in class when I returned wearing a cast and using crutches.

While in the hospital I met a local college student also receiving therapy for a broken leg, he was several years older. We ended up sharing a room and became buddies. He was like an older brother to me during that time and we'd talk about anything and everything. He'd just finished a drug rehab program and told me all about his previous addiction and the time he spent in rehab. He also told me stories about the many different people he met in rehab and their reasons for drug abuse. One in particular was a homosexual who confided in his parents and they couldn't understand it so they kicked him out of their house; as a result, he started experimenting with drugs, became addicted, and ended up in rehab. When I heard that story, I wanted more than anything to talk to my new friend about my own feelings and infatuations with men because he appeared so understanding of that other guy in rehab. Finally I had the opportunity to talk to someone older and someone I'd probably never see again in my life; that time I wasn't going to let the opportunity pass me by.

A couple days before I was to be released from the hospital I talked to my roommate and told him about my infatuation with men. He asked if my parents knew. I told him they didn't and he said it might be best to keep it that way. He told me he had a couple college friends who were homosexuals and that while he didn't totally understand their sexual preferences, he accepted them. He said he believed a person could change through heterosexual dating and eventual marriage, with that change occurring gradually. Not knowing anything different at the time, I believed what he said and decided to accept the fact time would tell for me.

I finally got home from the hospital and returned to school. Sure enough, when I went back to my driving education class, the instructor came up to me and said breaking my leg was a stupid thing to do; he slapped me up the side of my head. At least he didn't tell me I'd have to take the class over. Upon completion of the class I took a written test and received a driving permit to drive with a licensed driver. Later that school year, I took the actual driving part of the exam and received my full legal driving license.

LIVING THE DIFFERENCE

Believe it or not breaking my leg, meeting a special new friend, and obtaining my driving license ended up being the highlights of my sophomore year. I had hopes my upcoming junior year would bring more excitement and leave more of a lasting impact.

The summer between my sophomore and junior year was a drag. I worked most the summer for the same janitorial cleaning service. A few times that summer my dad would let me take his car; I'd gather up some friends and we'd go to a drive in movie. The only real lasting impact the summer had was on my checkbook; I practically worked myself to death.

The new school year began and I was a junior in high school. I had to take PE class the first semester because it was a requirement to graduate. I had the same problem with the class as I did in junior high, except the guys were more mature and physically more developed; it was much more difficult to keep my eyes off many of them. You'll never guess who taught that PE class!

The second semester started and I was finished with PE, thank God! I was worried the entire first semester I'd get slapped up the side of my head while I was trying to keep things under control in the shower room. Yes, the PE instructor was the coach that taught my driving education class the previous year.

The year passed by quickly. In one of my classes there was a good looking new student who sat in front of me and I had a terribly difficult time not starring at him. He was somewhat quiet and shy which made him all the more attractive to me. I kept remembering in the back of my mind what my friend in the hospital told me earlier, so I worked hard at ignoring the new student; it was difficult, but I tried. Finally I decided it's not going to hurt anybody if I did sneak a peek or two. While I was sneaking those peeks, I was told by another classmate that someone was taking their own peeks at me; it was a girl.

It was about a month before the high school prom and the peeking girl came up to me after class asking if I'd go to the prom with her. I hadn't really given a thought to attending the prom, but since she asked I told her yes. The month flew by and the prom was upon us. I did all the normal preparations like buying her a corsage and buying some new dress slacks for me, along with a sport coat. I hadn't bought my own car yet. With the family car being so old and not cool to drive, I convinced my sister to let me use her new car the evening of the prom. I was rather excited for that evening and proud of myself for mustering up the courage to actually go to the prom, especially with a girl; however, had she not asked, I probably wouldn't have been going!

I went to pick her up and her father put me through the third degree. I evidently passed his inspection because he allowed me to pin the corsage on her dress and let her walk out the door with me. I was wondering the entire time what her folks thought of me. Like I said before, I didn't consider myself a *queer*, but I still worried they'd think I was different in some way. Different or not, we went out to dinner that evening with some other class-mates and had a nice time. There was a little time after dinner before the actual prom dance began so we dragged main. That was the thing to do in those days; it took a lot of gas, but we were only paying about thirty cents a gallon then. About an hour of doing that was enough and we went on to the dance.

I hadn't danced before so I looked at others on the dance floor and began to fling my arms around and move my legs like everyone else seemed to be doing. I must have danced ok as she asked me where I learned to dance. You don't think she meant that in another way do you? The dance came to an end and I took her home; I walked with her to the front door and gave her a goodnight kiss. I had no idea if we'd ever go out again.

A few weeks into summer I decided to give her a call and ask if she wanted to take in a movie. She did and we went to the drive in theater. I didn't know how far or if I should make any moves on her; heck, I didn't know if I actually wanted to or even could make any moves. I didn't have to wonder long as she made the first move; aggres-sive little thing she was! We had a nice evening and started to date regularly after that.

That summer we introduced our parents to each oth-er. We went on several dates and I truly enjoyed the time we spent together; however, there was never the warm inner feeling I thought should come over me whenever we'd hug or kiss, like I'd get whenever I was infatuated with a man. Naturally I hid that fact from her and we continued to date. I placed a tremendous amount of reliance on what I'd previously been told about change occurring gradually.

Well, there it was, our senior year in high school was about to begin. We were still dating and tried to get most of our classes together. While I was still waiting on that gradual change to commence, she was becoming very serious. The discussion of marriage even came up and I was beginning to feel pressured. We had our ups and downs throughout the year, but still remained a couple.

I did buy my own car that year and boy was it nice. I purchased a brand new Plymouth Gold Duster; it was the top of the duster line from Plymouth. It had a half vinyl top, mag wheels, sporty stripes running along the sides, and of course, split bench sport seats. I paid for it myself and my dad paid the insurance on it. I was very proud of it.

It was a fun year. College career days came around and there were representatives from several colleges and universities. My girlfriend and I decided to attend college close to home to save on living expenses. We'd each be able to live at home the first year and commute to classes; the reason for my saying first year is that it looked more and more like we'd be getting married the summer after our first college year and I prayed to

God a large portion of that gradual change would take place before that time. As it turned out, several of our classmates decided on the same college and when it was time to enroll for our freshman year, we coordinated our schedules in order that we could car pool to classes saving even more.

Our senior prom night was fantastic. We had a banquet early in the evening served to us by the junior class. A dance followed and everyone seemed to dance the night away; I was a much better dancer that time around. We attended an all night showing of movies at the drive in arranged by our high school sponsors. Everything seemed to be going great with everyone having a fantastic time, everyone except me! You must understand, while I was having a good time and definitely caught up in the moment, a part of me kept saying to myself, "Who am I trying to fool?" I was still infatuated with men, there was no feeling of a gradual change taking place within me, and I had recent conversations with a girl about marriage.

AN EARLY DREAM REALIZED MUCH LATER IN LIFE

LIVING THE DIFFERENCE

I slept the entire next day and when I finally did wake up I vividly remembered a dream that occurred. I dreamt about a wedding; I was getting married, except it wasn't to a girl, it was to the guy who sat ahead of me my junior year. It was the guy I couldn't keep my eyes off of. Was a change ever going to take place or at least begin? Was I ever going to have dreams about women?

It was 1973 and I graduated from high school; as screwed up as I was, I graduated and I might add with honors! What a roller coaster ride my life had been to that point; I didn't have to go to an amusement park to catch the ride, I was continually on it!

Summer began and it'd be the last summer before becoming a big man on campus, a college campus. I also moved up that summer, moved up from working as a janitor to working as a clothing salesman in a high end clothing store. I really enjoyed it and had a terrific boss. The new job was good for me because not only was I continually exposed to new and exciting people, but I had an inside first look at the latest in clothing trends and fashion. I didn't take home much money during the first few weeks of employment because I spent most of my paychecks on clothes. That was ok though; I wanted to look my best when I started college in the fall. Another great thing about the new job was I'd be able to work whenever I didn't have classes, as well as weekends and holiday breaks from college.

There I was a freshman in college. Having always liked

school, college was no different. That first year I loaded up on classes because I wanted to graduate with a double major in accounting and business administration. Had I known then what I know now, as far as my current hobbies, likes, and dislikes, I'd have concentrated my studies in architecture or journalism. I remember one of the first essays I wrote for an English class, the professor told me I had a definite talent for writing. I never gave it a second thought at the time.

Classes were a blast; my goal was to get as much out of every class I could and ace them all. Since I was paying for my own college education, I wanted to earn as many scholarships as possible and the best way to do that was to excel in school. The first semester I received an A in every class and earned a scholarship for the second semester.

The semester also produced another result, my girlfriend and I decided to get engaged and marry the following summer. Still remembering back to what my friend in the hospital told me, I thought it was the right thing to do and just maybe it'd jump start that gradual change in my inner feelings. I definitely had a feeling of love for her, but it wasn't the type of love it should've been. I prayed to God it'd develop into the proper form of love.

I bought an engagement ring that semester and asked her to marry me. She immediately said yes and it was official. Her parents wanted us to wait and marry when we graduated from college, they thought we might not finish if married earlier. My parents were ecstatic and couldn't wait until we got married. Thinking back, I've often wondered if my parents saw the difference in me and assumed marriage would change me. We ended up setting the date for early summer.

The second semester flew by, most likely in part to all the wedding preparations going on at the time. Nothing too exciting occurred that semester, other than knocking out a few more general education courses. Before I knew it, the semester was over and it was wedding bells around the corner. My feet were frigid; however, I stayed the course.

It was Saturday, June 8, 1974, family and friends were gathered at the church. I was extremely nervous, yet somewhat excited. I was about to begin a new journey in life that could change my life immensely and set me on the straight and narrow so to speak! I don't think I cracked a smile during the entire ceremony or at least that's what the wedding photos revealed. The day was beautiful and everyone appeared to enjoy the festivities.

Before the reception was over we left on our honeymoon. We stopped along our way to Colorado and spent the first night in New Mexico. I was getting real fidgety; I looked for every excuse to put off getting in bed with my new wife. I even went out looking for a grocery store to pick up some things for the ice chest. Then I went to the carwash to clean the shaving cream off the car. Finally it was time to take her to bed; without going into details, I'll just say I was able to perform under pressure.

NEXT FEW CORNERS

We arrived home in a few days and life pretty much went back to normal. We lived in married student housing on campus and would be able to walk back and forth to classes. We kept our jobs and worked full time the remainder of the summer, then went part time when classes began in the fall. I was real excited for the new semester as I'd be able to begin some classes actually within my field of study, along with the balance of the general education courses.

My sophomore year in college went by fast. I overloaded my class schedule and with my studies and work, stayed extremely busy. At the time, college requirements included necessary credits for PE; you know what that involved! That time it didn't mean showering with a group of guys. One could enroll in tennis, bowling, dance classes, and many other classes to satisfy the credits. I was able to satisfy my PE credits without once having to shower with the guys, which was a good thing because one of the guys I played tennis with was, as one would say today, hot. Yes, I still had that infatuation with men; any changes I'd expected to occur hadn't begun.

Late the following summer my wife and I took a trip to South Dakota. I wanted to introduce her to friends and relatives living there and not in attendance at our wedding; no, I didn't introduce her to my croquet buddy. We had a nice trip and saw many of my aunts and uncles that unbeknownst to me at the time would be the last time I'd see some of them. We arrived home and had to immediately get our class schedules worked out for the new school year about to begin.

We celebrated our first wedding anniversary that summer with family and friends, our first year of marriage turned out to be ok. I really felt comfortable around her parents by that time and no longer worried they thought I might be different. I continually worked on those feelings, infatuations, fixations, or whatever they were as I was fairly sure at that point they weren't going to gradually change on their own.

The new school year began and I was a junior. I joined and participated in a lot of extracurricular activities that year. One in particular was an honor society I was invited to join; not only did I join, but was elected an officer for the year. As such, I qualified as a delegate to the regional convention.

Later in the school year I went to the convention with the other delegates from our school. I met many students from colleges and universities throughout the region. There were various meetings on the convention agenda; however, we weren't expected to attend them all. At one of the meetings I was the only delegate from our school; the meeting was extremely short and I had some time before the next group of meetings began. While I was killing time, I came upon a small group of students talking in the corridor; I stood there a moment finally realizing they were discussing forming a group on each of their campuses to deal with the problems and the discrimination of gays on campus. I didn't know of any such problems on our campus, unless I was blind to that fact because I worked so hard at distancing myself from gays. I quickly walked away from the group before the other meetings let out so I wouldn't run into anyone I knew.

My junior year was fun. I was also selected outstanding student by the professors in the School of Business Administration. I continued to pull an *A* in every class and received additional forms of scholarships. My streak finally came to an end when my business law professor had a policy of not giving out a single *A* to anyone, even if a student had excellent work; I received a *B* in his class! I always felt I needed to prove myself, most likely arising from some subconscious thought due to my screwed up sexual preferences.

The summer between my junior and senior year was fairly uneventful except for one thing. One day a classmate from an earlier business class came to the clothing store where I worked and wanted me to take a quick break. We'd previously worked on a school project together so I didn't give the request a second thought. We went across the street to order something to drink and he asked if I ever went the other way. Honestly, at that point in my life, I hadn't a clue as to what he meant; call me naïve, but I really didn't! I said, "What do you mean?" and he answered, "You know, mess around with a guy." I was shocked because I knew he was married. I told him I didn't do things like that. He asked if I'd ever thought about it and I told him I really needed to get back to work. We both left and went our separate ways.

You have no idea how close I came to accepting his proposition. My inner feelings were roused and a part of me was at attention ready to go, but I knew in my mind it wasn't the right thing to do. I was still anxiously awaiting a change to take place and I didn't want anything to mess that up.

Summer ended and I began my senior year in college. Wow, I would graduate soon and enter the world of the working class. I was selected that year to be included in *Who's Who Among Students in American Universities and Colleges*, an annual publication recognizing various students from across the country. I was also elected president of *Alpha Chi*, the honor society on campus. I had loads of fun that year and wanted to make a lasting impact on my last year of undergraduate studies. I wanted my mom and dad to be proud of me; I was going to be the only one in our immediate family to receive a four year college degree. While I had yet to achieve that normal feeling about myself, I did achieve a wonderful feeling about my academic achievements. Little consolation as that may seem to others in light of my screwed up feelings, it meant a lot to me!

Graduation day was upon me, family and friends were present. I graduated with honors and was ranked in the upper echelon of the graduating class; that one *B* from the business law professor kept me from graduating at the very top of the class. I wonder where he is today!

NEXT FEW CORNERS

The summer after graduation was full of frenzy and excitement. My wife was accepted to the *O. U. Health Sciences Center* in Oklahoma City to begin her studies in physical therapy and we needed to relocate by the start of the fall term. I immediately began sending out resumes to businesses and accounting firms in the Oklahoma City area in hopes of landing a position prior to relocation. I made several trips to Oklahoma City that summer on many different interviews; nothing of interest resulted in my job search and it appeared we'd be forced to relocate without jobs. Maybe I was being overly selective, but I didn't want to accept just anything. We signed a lease on an apartment during one of our trips and went back home to begin packing. A few days prior to the actual move, I received a call from an accounting firm, not my choice of firms, and was offered a position. Of course I accepted and would continue my job search upon relocation. Our parents assisted in the move and we caravanned to Oklahoma City in what'd be the hottest day of the summer; it was a totally exhaustive trip.

My mom rode with me and it was just the two of us; we talked the entire trip. She was a talker, guess that's where I inherited my gift of gab. She asked if I was happy and naturally I told her yes. I really wanted to talk about my feelings, but I just couldn't. I loved my mother dearly and we were very close, I just couldn't chance hurting her with news about my sexual preferences. I knew in the bottom of my heart she'd understand, but I still held on to that glimmer of hope those preferences would gradually change.

We arrived, got everything unloaded, and went out to eat. Our parents spent the evening at a nearby hotel and we slept on the floor of the apartment. The next morning our parents came by prior to heading back and it was time to say goodbye. It was an extremely difficult time for me because I was so close to my parents; everyone ended up crying. We were only a five hour drive away, but it was the first time either of us had been that far from our parents.

4

Early Career

My early career began without much fanfare. The accounting firm I worked for was very small and career advancement didn't look promising in that firm. I continued my job search with hopes of landing a better career position. The only memorable event I can associate with that first position was the death of Elvis Presley; the receptionist at the office got sick and vomited when she heard the news.

I finally landed a position as an internal auditor with a large national finance company. While the position was located in Oklahoma City, I interviewed with the head of auditing from New York City. Ironically, there were three of us from that small accounting firm interviewing for the position; none of us knew the others had interviews until a couple weeks later when I went back to the firm and checked on the receptionist.

I began my new position and truly enjoyed the switch

from public accounting. There were two of us in the Oklahoma City internal auditing department and we occupied an office located within the accounting control center of the company, employing an additional fifty plus employees. I met a lot of new and interesting individuals, with one eventually becoming a lifelong friend who'd follow me into the banking business later in my career.

Meanwhile, my wife was busy with her school and worked weekends in a small suburban hospital. I was quite bored on weekends and had to look for things to do; living in a small apartment in a new city made it much more challenging, especially since we only had one automobile and she drove it to work on the weekends. We did have a little dog and I'd take her for long walks when the weather was nice, that helped pass some of the time.

One Saturday morning I walked to a nearby convenience store to buy a *Newsweek* or some other business magazine and lo and behold in the rack next to it was a magazine with a provocative semi-nude picture of a man on the cover. Of course that got my attention so I purchased it; I couldn't wait to get back to the apartment and flip through the magazine. Wow, it was full of pictures of naked men, along with numerous articles; I thought they might be newsworthy articles until I began reading and found them to be provocative stories involving fantasies. I was stunned a magazine like that existed; coming from a small town and a medium sized college campus, I hadn't been exposed to any gay magazines. I will say I was entertained for a few hours. I didn't want my wife to find the magazine so I pulled up the carpet in the corner of the spare bedroom closet and hid the magazine there for future reference. I wonder if it's still there!

Where was that gradual change that was supposed to take place, do you think my earlier friend from the hospital knew what he was talking about? I began to wonder. It was extremely difficult dealing with it all. Do you follow your hormonal instincts or do you strive to be someone you're not and may never be? I just didn't have that much needed feeling of fulfillment one needs; however, I hadn't given up yet even though my life was lacking.

I needed a change, something exciting! A change is what I got; the head of auditing from New York called and informed me I'd be traveling most of the coming year. The company had branches throughout much of the country and it'd been some time since anyone performed on site audits. That was fine with me; I was ready to leave that day. I spent the next several weeks performing preliminary work on the upcoming audits and preparing all the necessary working paper schedules for each branch.

The time came to leave for the branches. They were of distances that required air travel and I'd never been on an airplane; there were two of us from the Oklahoma City office going on the audits so at least I had company. One of the first branches was in the Carolinas; we changed airlines a couple times and ended up on a small twin engine plane. We were flying through the mountains when the pilot got on the intercom telling us we'd be landing momentarily I looked all around and saw only trees. I was starting to get nervous; before I knew it, the plane appeared to be chopping off the tree tops so I closed my eyes and started praying, in a few seconds we were on the ground. I about peed my pants; I didn't realize the airport was on a clearing high up in the mountains! That wasn't the type of excitement I was referring to earlier.

The next several months took me to all parts of the country on many different flights. I was having the time of my life visiting state after state, city after city, bar after bar; yes, at a few of the branches the managers enjoyed their liquor. After a long day at the branch office we'd go out to dinner and end up bar hopping. I hadn't really acquired a taste for liquor, but did enjoy an ice cold beer; it was a way to unwind and really get to know the personnel at the branches.

One of the places we bar hopped was in Chicago along *Rush Street*; it was where everyone congregated. One evening we finished dinner and walked down *Rush Street* stopping at a local bar for a drink; when we left one of the guys said we needed to go to another bar a few blocks away, he said it had the best sound system around and a very large dance floor. When we got there and went inside, I couldn't believe my eyes. There were guys dancing with guys, some of them even with their shirts off. They were dancing to disco music and I could feel the beat deep in my bones; a part of me wanted to get out there on the dance floor with them. I'd never been to a gay bar before. To this day, I don't know if he was gay or just wanted to expose some country hicks from Oklahoma to a gay bar.

EXPOSURE TO MY FIRST GAY BAR

LIVING THE DIFFERENCE

When I arrived back to the hotel I couldn't go to sleep. I kept thinking there's no way that many guys could be screwed up about their sexual preferences. I thought there's more to this than I'm aware of. I decided at that point I needed to perform some in depth research on homosexuality.

It wasn't long before the audits were complete. I spent the next few weeks finalizing the results and preparing a report for the head of auditing in New York. Just as I was preparing to mail the report, he called and wanted it hand delivered. Did this mean what I thought it meant? Sure enough, I was going to New York City.

Before I knew it, the time came to leave for New York City; it was a long flight with a couple stops along the way. When I arrived I took a cab from the airport to the hotel, it wasn't just any hotel it was the *New York City St. Moritz Hotel on the Park*. It was a Sunday evening and I arrived in time to take a leisurely stroll through central park. Wow, what a place! The park was full of people, all types of people; I wasn't apprehensive at all as it appeared totally safe to me. After my stroll, I went back to the hotel and ordered up room service. One of my favorite desserts at that time was cheesecake so I ordered a New York strip, a vanilla milkshake, and a frickin' New York style cheesecake with a drizzle of strawberry glaze on top. I was becoming quite the world traveler, fancy that! I spent the entire week in New York City, but only had limited time for sightseeing; that was ok, just being there was enough excitement to last a lifetime, or so I thought at the time.

Throughout all that my wife managed to graduate and find employment as a physical therapist. She even found the time to unpack and get us settled in the home we'd purchased between business trips; of course, I was home for her graduation and all the festivities. Since I'd be in the Oklahoma City office for a period, I decided to find the time and research homosexuality at the library.

I went to the library on several occasions reading many diverse articles and reviewing numerous studies relating to homosexuality. I had a lot to absorb and realized it appeared to be a complex subject matter with no clear-cut answers, at least none I'd find initially; I didn't like that, but I could accept it. My wife hadn't a clue I had those feelings so the research was kept quiet.

Life went on and my wife and I decided to start a family. It was something we both definitely wanted. I'd always enjoyed being around children and couldn't wait to have some of my own. She stopped the pill and we began working on it; those pressure performances came around real fast. We weren't in any hurry, just whenever it happened.

In a few months I was informed I'd have an assignment in Chicago coming up soon, length of the assignment wasn't determinable at the time. The company had a subsidiary there experiencing some problems and the office in New York was putting a team together to go out to deal with it. It was a totally separate part of the business and had nothing to do with my previous trip to Chicago.

The time came and I was off to Chicago. It was bitterly cold when I arrived. There were several of us there; I was the only one from Oklahoma City with the rest from New York City. We stayed at the *Downtown Chicago Marriott on Michigan Avenue*; it hadn't been open long and was quite a showplace. The assignment lasted an extended time and all of us became good friends. We'd fly home on weekends to be with our families and then back on Sunday nights to prepare for the new work week.

One guy in particular became a very close friend of mine. He lived with his parents in an apartment in New York City. We were close in age, but he had so much more experience under his belt in all areas, probably from growing up in New York City. We did everything together outside the Chicago office, sometimes with the others and sometimes just the two of us. We were buddies. I found myself becoming attracted to him and I didn't know what to do; I didn't get any sense he was gay, so I kept quiet. I was still confused about the entire homosexuality issue and prayed for an answer; I even thought once there were children in the family, a change would occur. I had a difficult time working with him the remainder of the assignment because of my attraction to him, but somehow I managed to keep things under control.

The assignment ended and I was back in Oklahoma City to stay. I thoroughly enjoyed my position with the company, but realized there was no future without a move to New York City. I didn't consider that for a moment. I had a decision to make, stay with the company and continue traveling whenever assignments came up or start sending out resumes. Since my wife and I were trying to start a family, traveling was out of the equation; I started circulating my resume.

I mailed out well over one hundred resumes in an all out effort to find not only a new position, but a fantastic career move at the same time. I received a tremendous response resulting in several interviews. I remember receiving a few good offers and finally decided on an offer from the holding company of one of the largest banks in Oklahoma City. The decision felt right.

We continued to try for some time and no baby. Of course I naturally thought I was being punished for my sexual preferences, so I decided to see a doctor and have some testing done. There wasn't a problem with my guys, so at that time we started to consider adoption. My mom was adopted and there was a special place in my heart for the entire adoption process; I started to get real excited. We visited with various adoption agencies and the average wait time was three to five years, even with special needs children; that seemed like eternity so we decided to go the private route. We contacted our family physician back home and informed him of our intention to adopt. It then became a waiting game.

Meanwhile, my new career in banking was taking

off. I met a lot of new people and got settled in rather quick. It was a diverse group of individuals I met; my first hunch was some of the employees were definitely closeted. A group of us would meet every morning in the bank cafeteria for biscuits and gravy. There was one particular individual who was always making comments about homosexuals. It appeared he'd do it to see the expression on our faces; I was good at concealing my reaction to such conversation, I'd done it my entire life. One individual wasn't so good at it, eventually he quit going to breakfast with us and eventually left the bank. It was sad there was so much discrimination against homosexuals; it existed everywhere. Ironically, several years later I ran into that individual who'd made those comments; it was at a gay bar! He told me he was only there to check out the new sound system the club had recently installed; what a jerk, they even exist among the gay population.

In a short time, I was handed additional responsibilities and after several months, a promotion came my way. The promotion was heading up the accounting and financial reporting for one of the subsidiaries of the bank holding company. It was a great opportunity with a chance to broaden and expand my knowledge into the mortgage banking business. I spent many nights and weekends shaping the department into what was needed; part of the shaping was realigning certain personnel and hiring a new assistant. I went through a few assistants during the first couple years before I found one with the drive and determination it took to succeed in the position, not knowing at the time my new assistant would turn out to be gay!

Throughout that time, we sold our first home and purchased a new home in a school district perfect for starting a family. After just a few months in our new home we heard from our family physician, a child would be available for adoption soon. The natural mother was in the final couple months of her pregnancy. We were so excited we didn't know exactly what all we needed to do, we were going to have our first baby!

On November 17, 1982, I received a telephone call at my office informing me our son was born and we could go pick him up that evening. I was so excited I couldn't speak; I ran around the office trying to tell everyone I had to leave to go pick up my newborn son, I don't think they understood a word I said. The bundle of joy wasn't even a day old when we took him in our arms; it was one of the happiest days in my life!

Business was growing and everything appeared to be running smooth. I still had those moments of infatuation with men, but I was determined more than ever to overcome them. I prayed most every day the change I'd been waiting for my entire life would start to take place. I kept waiting and waiting and waiting and waiting! I was happy with my career, content with my wife, and extremely happy with my son; there was just a void in my life. I went to see a psychiatrist; he too said I could change so

I continued working on it and giving it time. I guess I needed that reassurance.

Before I realized it over a year had passed. We received another telephone call from our family physician and he thought we'd want a brother for our first son; I was ecstatic and couldn't wait for another child. I'd have two sons, what more could a guy want; I had that reassurance from my psychiatrist that a change could eventually take place and I was being blessed with another son.

On August 23, 1984, we received the telephone call we'd been waiting on, our second son was born; however, he was premature and it'd be a few days before we'd be able to pick him up. I could barely work those few days as I was so anxious to pick up my son and I couldn't concentrate on anything. We went out and bought the smallest baby outfit we could find since he was premature. When we picked him up from the hospital, the nurse dressed him in the outfit and he wriggled right out of it. He was the smallest little guy I'd ever seen; I couldn't wait to hold my new son. Again, I was experiencing one of the happiest days in my life!

My sons were growing up extremely fast. Every day I could see them change right before my eyes; I'd get home from the office and one or both of them would've done something new and entirely different that day. My wife always arrived home in the evenings before I did and she'd practically be at the door waiting to tell me everything.

Our parents visited their grandchildren quite frequently.

The visits were always extremely fun times. I remember one of the visits we took everyone out to eat at a Mexican restaurant the day they arrived. Keep in mind my youngest son was only a couple years old at that time. We were all sitting around a large table talking about what the boys had done and how fast they were growing. Finally a waiter came to the table and asked if everyone was ready to place their order; the waiter was Hispanic. The first one to say anything was my youngest son, be blurted out, "Se se senor!" My oldest son started to giggle; by that time both of the boys were practically rolling on the floor giggling and carrying on. Everyone started to laugh including the waiter. Times like that will always occupy a special place in my heart!

In the meantime, I kept busy at the office and before long the business outlook wasn't good. Of course with Oklahoma being the energy state it was and currently still is, the bank had many of their eggs in that basket at the time, when that sector of the economy began a downward spiral, it was felt tremendously in the banking industry. As a result, decisions had to be made and courses altered to compensate for the prevailing business climate. The residential and commercial areas of the mortgage banking business went their own ways; I ended up remaining with the commercial area that was still part of the bank holding company. Our office was eventually moved from downtown and relocated to a prime new commercial development; however, residency at that location lasted a short time as further deterioration of the business climate necessitated a move back downtown to the main bank building.

Throughout all that my nerves were getting the best of me and I went to see a different psychiatrist. My infatuation with men remained and was getting stronger as time went on. I tried so hard to change those feelings, but it just didn't happen. By that time it wasn't just a question as to if a change could take place, it was also whether a change would actually take place. I told my new psychiatrist what I was told by a friend many years before and subsequently confirmed by a previous visit to a different psychiatrist. He was stunned, he said the other psychiatrist should have his license to practice taken away. He told me it wasn't a choice, that medical studies have proven so. He assured me God made me that way, not by accident or choice, it just happened! He went on to say it must be a living nightmare trying to be someone I could never be. I thought my life was going to end! I continued my therapy with him for several sessions, while keeping the entire situation between the two of us. During that time of therapy, I performed additional research at the library with the assistance and guidance of my psychiatrist.

REALIZING WHAT I'D KNOWN FOR A VERY LONG TIME

LIVING THE DIFFERENCE

Watching my sons grow and keeping extremely busy at the office kept my mind somewhat on track. Personally, I didn't know what to; I wanted my family more than ever and wanted to be the husband my wife needed me to be, yet at the same time, I had a void in my life gnawing away at me.

Things were continuing to worsen on the business front and bank failures were becoming headline stories. I kept the momentum going at the office, not only for me, but for the employees as well. Little by little, anyone that left for whatever reason, we wouldn't replace them; if needed we'd use temps. We arrived at the point where we had more temps than permanent employees. I was even selected client of the quarter by the temps I employed through one of the larger local agencies. I thought many times I needed to jump ship, but there was no place to go.

One evening I was working late and received a call from one of my close friends at another subsidiary. He and his wife lived a short distance from our neighborhood and had become friends of ours; we were racquetball buddies at the time. His office was a couple floors above mine and he'd previously mentioned to me in confidence the rumor the bank was on the brink of collapse. That evening he told me to look out my window at the street below; sure enough we were being taken over, the bank had failed! I immediately telephoned my wife telling her what was happening; it'd be some time before I made it home that evening.

EARLY CAREER

The holding company was still intact, which wasn't saying much at the time as one of their larger holdings, the bank, had just failed. I ended up being the last employee of the commercial business and remained on board with the holding company to assist in various areas of their remaining business; I eventually moved across the street to the holding company headquarters. I knew my position had limited life at that point and immediately began circulating resumes, not only locally, but nationally as well. With the Oklahoma economy in the shape it was at the time, there were no local positions to be found. Any position that might surface would have hundreds of unemployed professionals vying for it.

I ended up going on several out of town interviews throughout the country; I even had a couple offers, which of course meant relocating. That was a difficult option to consider at the time; I was still in therapy and had no idea what my own personal future would entail. I couldn't move my entire family across the country with that much uncertainty and take them away from their current and comfortable surroundings. My sons were the brightest spot in my life at the time and I couldn't do that to them; to keep the family together and close to relatives was still my priority.

My position at the holding company finally ended and for the first time in my early career, I was without a position. I collected unemployment for a time along with numerous other unemployed professionals and eventually ended up giving network marketing a try. In the meantime, I continued with my local job search.

What about my being gay? Yes, I knew I was; I knew I couldn't change that fact. I'm sure a part of me knew all along I was gay; I just had to exhaust all possibilities. So what was my next step? Could I live a lie the rest of my life? Would God want me to live a lie? What would my parents think? What would my sons think? What would this do to my wife? At the time, I didn't think I could handle coming out of the closet, I didn't know if others could handle it, so I kept my feelings locked up inside me.

The local job search produced no results; there weren't even any interviews to go on. So I spent most my time trying to build the network marketing business. I went to meeting after meeting, rally after rally; my wife even got involved. There were tapes to listen to and books to read. There was even a video on network marketing and my sons loved to watch it. I continued with the network marketing efforts for quite some time; ended up enrolling several people in my down line. I worked very hard at it, probably even harder than most anything up to that point in my life; of course, with the exception of trying to change my sexual preferences, that was the most work I'd ever put into anything. It didn't seem to matter how much time I put into building the network, the monetary rewards were just not there. Thinking back now, part of it could easily have been my own drive; with so many feelings locked up inside me, my driving force was definitely affected.

EARLY CAREER

My sons appeared to be very happy; my wife appeared not to be! I asked her what was wrong one evening and her reply indicated she was just stressed over the job situation. I decided then I needed to do something about the entire situation; with my wife being stressed and my own insides full of locked up feelings, it wouldn't be long before it could start affecting our sons. I even wondered at the time if just maybe my wife knew about my locked up feelings.

5

What Next

Other than sexual preferences, I really hadn't a clue what being gay was all about. Besides wanting to be with a man, I didn't really consider myself different from others. I finally decided one day I needed to find out just what the hoopla attached to being gay was all about.

There was a place in Oklahoma City known for meeting other gays. I went there a few times and met some other gay men. Ironically, many of the men I met were married and had a family. They were going through the same ordeal I was; it was refreshing to talk with them. For once, I could opening and honestly talk about my feelings with other men experiencing the very same feelings for men. I immediately felt some of those locked up feelings were finally getting some fresh air. However, I was surprised to find so many individuals in total complete denial; they still had a ways to go to catch up to the point where I was at with total awareness and near total acceptance of my own feelings.

Awareness, denial, and acceptance, they all go hand in hand; anyone questioning their own sexual preferences goes through the different levels in varying degrees of completeness and timeliness. It can drag on for a very long time, with some it can take their entire life before they're to the point of total acceptance, others may never reach that point and be in complete denial forever.

One of the guys I met told me about a support group for married men attempting to come out. I went to the next scheduled meeting and was surprised at the number of people in the room. There were guys from all walks of life such as attorneys, doctors, educators, legislatures, other white collar workers, blue collar workers, unemployed individuals, and many others. I got all choked up when I heard various individuals talk about their own experiences and quickly realized I wasn't actually abnormal.

When I got home that evening my wife said it must have been a good network meeting because I was in such a great mood. I'd lied to her; a network meeting was the reason I gave for leaving the house that evening. I decided to become more knowledgeable in all aspects of gay life before coming out to her.

Part of becoming more knowledgeable in the aspects of gay life meant becoming familiar with words and terms used in the gay community; I wanted to know what someone meant, regardless of their being a homosexual (gay) or heterosexual (straight), when they referred to a certain term or phrase in their conversations about gay life or gays in general. I was clueless certain words in the American language had attached to them special meanings when used in reference to the gay community, nor did I realize one could offend someone by innocently using the wrong word or term in reference to them. It was going to be more difficult when I did come out to my wife unless I was totally prepared with the terminology.

I realize some of you reading this book may need that same education. Before I go any further I want to define, in my own personal way, certain words and terms I feel will be of great benefit to your total enjoyment of my story. There's no specific order of importance and the following list is by no means all inclusive:

Gay- **term used to define an individual with sexual preferences directed to members of the same sex**

Lesbian- **term used to define sexual and romantic desires between females**

Dike- **slang term for lesbian**

Straight- **term used to define an individual with sexual preferences directed to members of the opposite sex**

LIVING THE DIFFERENCE

Homosexual- an individual with sexual preferences directed to members of the same sex

Heterosexual- an individual with sexual preferences directed to members of the opposite sex

Bisexual- an individual sexually confused with deep seated inhibitions in dealing with truly identifying their sexual preferences

Closeted- an individual having yet to admit their homosexuality to themselves or others

Coming Out- the process, understanding, and acceptance of being a homosexual and describing the same to others

Homophobia- fear of homosexuals and their corresponding lifestyle and culture

Civil Unions- a substitute for legal marriage in some states; while it has a legal status, the benefits are less than those of a full legal marriage

Domestic Partnerships- gay couples who reside in the same house; a legal status carrying few if any benefits

Butch- word used to define a gay man who is masculine in appearance and mannerisms

WHAT NEXT

Nelly- word used to define a gay man who is feminine in appearance and mannerisms

Diva- a sometimes arrogant and strong willed gay man who presents himself with an overabundance of confidence; also a drag queen with the same characteristics

Drag Queen- a gay man who dresses and assumes the characteristics and appearance of a woman; entertainers in full female dress who perform by dancing, singing, or lip syncing

Cross Dressers- anyone, homosexual or heterosexual, who identify themselves with the identity of the opposite sex by dressing and adapting their behavior to that sex; the term transvestite is many times given cross dressers incorrectly and when used is considered extremely defamatory

Drag Show- an entertainment show usually featuring drag queens and cross dressers who perform by dancing, singing, or lip syncing; many shows are purely for entertainment, while others involve fundraising to assist in and promote a worthy cause

Fag- used along with the terms queer, queen, and fairy when describing certain gay men who are extremely flamboyant and feminine; the term is offensive to many homosexuals and considered derogatory

Bear- word used to describe a gay man with an over-abundance of facial and body hair

Cub- word used to describe a smaller or younger bear; many times a bottom

Otter- word used to describe a real thin or skinny bear

Wolf- word used to describe an otter that is very aggressive

Bottom- the penetrated partner during gay anal sex

Top- the penetrating partner during gay anal sex

Sodomy- sex between two men involving an act of anal intercourse

Oral Sex- sex between two men involving the oral stimulation of the sex organs

While I was acquainting myself with the gay world, I continually put my foot in my mouth many times due to my ignorance of the terminology. I needed an education;

WHAT NEXT

I was determined to fit in and adapt to the new world I knew I'd eventually become a part of.

In the meantime, finding a position of employment was still among my top priorities of the time. I decided at that time to try a new approach in my job search. I hired an outplacement firm that virtually guaranteed with their assistance I'd be back working in my profession within six to eight months. Not only did I pay them an enormous sum of money for their assistance, but I also invested a tremendous amount of time going through their program and following all the guidelines they recommended. Even though I had ample time, I began to realize after just a short time in the program, I'd be the one doing everything to land a position; my initial consultation with the outplacement firm was extremely misleading as to how and what they'd do in assisting me with that goal. After all was said and done, their services offered little value to my search.

I was still getting my foot in the door of the gay community. I regularly stopped in at a local center dedicated to assistance for and education of individuals attempting to come out. I'd attend various meetings dealing with an array of subject matters. At one meeting in particular there was an extremely nice female who befriended me. We went for coffee after the meeting and she totally blew me away with her story. I thought she was one hundred percent female in every personal and biological aspect; however, she was a *drag queen*. She wasn't in full female dress; she looked like your average everyday housewife in everyday clothing. I couldn't believe my eyes and honestly didn't know whether I should or even could believe her. Before we left, she wanted to prove she was actually a he so we went to the restroom and she stood at the urinal draining her bladder in the same way I relieved myself; what a startling revelation!

She was an extremely nice person and appeared to possess a significant amount of intelligence. She told me she'd always considered herself a women, not a man and definitely not gay. She wanted surgery to correct the biological mishap, but would have to wait until she saved enough money to have it performed. She didn't want to be a man in a relationship with a woman or in a relationship with another man; she wanted to be a woman in a relationship with a man. I remember telling her I wished a surgery existed to change the inner feelings of a man wanting to remain a man and wanting to be with and attracted to other men. Of course the two are an entirely different set of circumstances and no such surgery exists for the latter.

We kept in touch; I received a telephone call from her one afternoon and she was distraught and extremely upset. She told me she'd met a wonderful man and had been dating him a few weeks; she thought she was falling in love with him. She went on to say he hadn't a clue she was actually a man. Having already gone through the preliminary steps prior to the sex change surgery, she'd (I always referred to her as a woman as that's how I saw her) already developed breasts like a woman; she told him she couldn't go all the way until she was married. She'd already met his family and they thought the two of them were a perfect match. She wanted my advice on what to do next. I told her she was asking the wrong person; however, I did tell her she was playing a risky game and a lot of emotions were at stake with a lot of people standing a chance of being deeply hurt.

I didn't hear back from her for some time; when I finally did, she mentioned she leveled with her boyfriend completely and he wanted time to think and decide if he could handle the situation. She asked if I'd mind her giving out my telephone number and somewhat reluctantly, I said it'd be fine. In a few days I received a telephone call from her boyfriend and it was an extremely awkward conversation. He was definitely in love with her, but was afraid to commit until she had the sex change; he wanted to see for himself if the surgery would in fact completely render her a woman in his mind. I never heard back from either of them.

During my process of self education to the gay world, I came across a telephone number in the telephone book; it was a gay crisis hotline. Not that I was in a crisis mode, but I decided to call it one day anyway; on the other end was a very nice gentleman who'd eventually become one of my best friends in life. We'd talked for several minutes when he said he needed to catch callers from the other lines. I gave him my telephone number and received a call back later in the day. We went for coffee that evening and he proved extremely knowledgeable in every aspect of homosexuality; I found a wealth of knowledge in what he shared with me. In time we not only became best friends, but I'd meet his mother who'd become a second mom to me and a person I'd grow to love dearly.

In the meantime, I continued my job search, as well as additional exploration of the gay community. Ironically, I met a person in the gay community who needed assistance with accounting and tax work for a business he was about to open. I set up the office for his business including the proper accounting and financial reporting systems with all appropriate guidelines; additionally, I set up all required local, state, and federal tax account recording systems. I was somewhat killing two birds with one stone; he'd come out several years earlier and had a wealth of knowledge that proved beneficial in my eventual coming out.

I thought I knew him well; however, one evening proved otherwise. We went out to dinner to celebrate his business getting off the ground and heading toward what appeared to be a fantastic future; he invited me to his home afterward for a glass of wine. To this day, I only remember having one glass of wine; however, a couple hours after arriving at his home, I woke up and realized I'd been raped. He was no where in sight so I quickly put myself together and drove home. Many thoughts were going through my mind; I couldn't go to the police nor could I tell my wife what happened. I hadn't even come out to her at that point and news like that would surely have devastated her. I decided then I couldn't put off coming out any longer. I needed to totally and unequivocally accept who and what I was.

DATE RAPE CAN HAPPEN TO ANYONE

LIVING THE DIFFERENCE

I set up what I hoped would be my last appointment with my psychiatrist, at least that particular one. I wanted some reassurance what I was about to do was the right thing to do. Of course I knew he wouldn't directly tell me that, but I still needed to talk. I was in his office for a two hour session; some of the time I just sat there and didn't say a word, the rest the time I couldn't shut up. He was extremely understanding and comforting and while my decision would have an affect on so many people, I felt deep in my heart I had his approval in going forward. I truly felt it was the right thing to do for everyone, including my wife and sons.

6

Coming Out

I continued to meet new and exciting people, not only in the gay community, but also in the business world, with some serious overlapping. Many would become lifelong friends, while others would be brief encounters. One in particular would become more; it was time to come out to my wife.

All I could think and say to myself was, "Where do I begin?" My coming out ended up being an extremely long drawn out process. I didn't just wake up one day deciding I was gay and tell the entire world about it; I didn't let anyone persuade, enlist, or convert me as I've heard some people actually believe can happen. As you have read to this point, basically my entire life has dealt with the process of coming out.

The time had come, it was Thanksgiving week 1988, circumstances were such we'd be staying in Oklahoma

City and not driving home to our parents to spend the holiday. A couple evenings prior to Thanksgiving, the boys were in bed early and I told my wife I needed to tell her something that'd be extremely difficult for both of us to talk about. She was totally caught off guard and wanted to know what it was. I told her I was gay! She didn't say anything for a moment and finally said, "No you're not!" "Are you sure?" she asked. I replied, "I've tried my entire life to overcome the feelings and have failed to overcome them." I told her I'd researched homosexuality until I was blue in the face; I also told her about my sessions with the psychiatrist. I wanted her to know it wasn't just a phase I was going through. I told her God made me that way and I couldn't live a lie any longer. She didn't believe that and told me I could change.

We talked a very long time; I could see she wasn't able to accept it that readily and definitely not that evening. We decided to quit talking about it for the evening; she said she was extremely confused, very tired, and wanted to go to bed. She went on to bed in the master bedroom and I went to the boys' room sleeping on the floor between their two beds. I don't believe I slept a wink all night and began to second guess myself as to whether I was doing the right thing.

The next morning was awkward; nothing was said to each other, we both went about our own business as usual and the boys went on to kindergarten and pre-school. That evening after dinner, after the boys went to bed, we talked again. She told me she thought about it her entire day at work and still thought I could change. I told her she might want to consider talking to a counselor or psychiatrist as I believed that'd open her mind to allow consideration of the research and studies relating to homosexuality. I knew her intelligence would prevail in the end; it had to be extremely difficult for her and I prayed God would assist in the process.

We decided I should live at home for the time being until we could work through everything; we didn't want to disrupt the boys' routine at the time. We also decided it best to tell the boys immediately we'd be separating soon so they wouldn't wonder why we'd be sleeping in separate bedrooms. We tried to keep as close to a constant regular routine as we possibly could under the circumstances.

Again, I could only imagine how difficult it all was for my wife. I was extremely concerned for my sons as well; however, I knew I was doing the right thing knowing there was an overabundance of love between us all and everyone would make it through the difficult times. By ending the lie I'd been living for so many years, I knew I'd become a better father for my sons and a better friend to my wife.

Eventually my wife did talk to a counselor; she told me he too said it wasn't a choice, homosexuals were born with those feelings and the feelings couldn't be changed. My wife was very stubborn at the time and while I knew she really had no choice but to accept my homosexuality in her mind she still thought I could change those feelings; that perception of mine was proven true by conversations after our subsequent divorce.

At that point, she was the only one I'd come out to; our families assumed we were going through an amicable divorce and nothing else. It'd be a little more time before I was ready to come out to my family and it was up to her if she ever wanted to tell hers; my sons were of the age that coming out to them at that time wouldn't have been wise. Amazingly enough, throughout all this my wife and I managed to remain good friends; we still are today. Sure we've had our differences, all divorced couples do, but I know in my heart she realizes I'd do anything for her as long as I possibly could!

It was becoming more difficult for me to remain in the house; it was just too awkward for everyone, including my sons. I started to look for a place of my own fairly close to the house so I'd be available should the family need anything. Apartments within close proximity to our house were extremely expensive at the time and I ended up signing a lease for an apartment a little further away. I somewhat took my time with the transition to the apartment as we'd decided in the meantime, after I'd signed the apartment lease, to sell our house and we wanted to coincide our moves off the property.

As mentioned earlier, one individual I'd met was becoming more than just a friend. We'd become extremely close and did a lot of things together. He eventually moved in and we shared the apartment. I wanted the family to meet him as I knew when I'd get the boys everyone would eventually cross paths; we had dinner together one evening and it went extremely well.

Time went on and things appeared to be going fine. My wife and I still hadn't finalized our divorce. I think she was still hoping in the back of her mind I was just going through a phase; I knew it wasn't because if it would've just been a phase, what I'm about to tell you wouldn't have hurt me so deeply. One evening when I returned home to the apartment, my close friend was there with someone else. It didn't take long for me to get him and his belongings out of the apartment; I was extremely hurt and disappointed with him. He was my first attempt at a gay relationship; I even hated him at the time for what he did!

Was that the life I wanted? I wasn't living a lie any longer, but I was really going through a tough time. I needed my parents and I needed to tell them everything. I called my mom and told her I really needed her and dad to come down for a visit. I told her I was really experiencing some severe anxiety. My dad was already retired so they were down within a couple days.

When my parents arrived I settled them in. We left shortly after their arrival to pick up my sons and then proceeded on to dinner; after dinner we dropped the boys back at their mothers and went back to the apartment. We just sat and didn't really say much at first. Dad asked what was bothering me and I could tell mom was about to break down in tears. I told them there was something I needed to tell them and they may not like what I was about to say. I said, "Mom and dad, I'm gay." Mom immediately cried out, "Thank God, I thought you were going to tell us you had cancer and was dying!" Dad said, "What do you want us to do?" I started to cry; they both moved closer to me and we hugged.

I told them everything and realized they'd probably known for some time. They told me my sister and her oldest daughter would be flying in from South Dakota; I truly believe mom thought my anxiety was due to some serious health issues and wanted others there. They arrived while my parents were still there and I came out all over again to everyone; I really couldn't tell how receptive to everything my sister was, I'd find out later she wasn't at all. I was getting pretty darn good at coming out by that time. I called my other sister to tell her as well and she said she'd known for years. The only one left in my family was my brother and I was scared to talk to him; I didn't want him to be disappointed with me. I called him one evening and we talked for some time; I wasn't quite as forthright with him as I was with everyone else, I thought it best to let him gradually become accustomed to it.

Everyone stayed for several days. We had a lot of fun together and included my sons as much as possible. I was even able to introduce my family to a few of my new friends; I wanted them to see they weren't freaks. I did keep the *fags*, *drag queens*, and *cross dressers* at bay though; thought that'd be a little much that early on!

The day I claimed my apartment back I decided to go to the shopping mall and buy something for myself. I was lonely after everyone left and thought that'd be a great lift in my spirits. Was I mistaken; I didn't even make it inside a store. When I walked in the mall I immediately saw an old friend from my banking days. I was batting a thousand as far as coming out to people and I was ready to step up to the plate again. I asked him if he wanted to go to the food court and get something to drink. It sounded great to him and after talking for about thirty minutes, I asked if he'd want to resume our racquetball games; we played during our banking days and always enjoyed it. It sounded like fun to him, so we decided to reserve a court for that coming weekend. Just as we got up from the table I told him I needed to mention something that I hoped wouldn't change our plans; I told him I was gay. I saw anger in his eyes, he punched me in the face and said, "Get away from me you frickin' *faggot*." I wasn't expecting that; my nose was bleeding so I went to the restroom for some paper towels. I finally stopped the bleeding and immediately went back to my apartment. I felt totally abused and ridiculed. What was one supposed to do in a situation like that? Should I've gone to mall security? Should I've called the police? Of course not, they could've been just as homophobic.

A CASUALTY OF BEING GAY

COMING OUT

Need I say that sort of did me in for the day; I went to bed early that evening and tried not to dwell on what happened. I realized at that point straight friends may not be as accepting as family members when it came to coming out, at least certain family members. I decided I needed to rethink my coming out strategy for the future.

There was still very little work to be found, only occasionally. I ended up going to work full time as the manager of a men's clothing store. I saw an advertisement in the local newspaper and went in to apply. I was surprised when I received a call back informing me I'd been selected for the position. Even though it was out of my chosen field, I was thrilled to be working full time again. I did have that experience from my college days when I worked part time in the local men's clothing store back home. I really enjoyed my new position even though the money wasn't what I was accustomed to; it was a paycheck. I wouldn't be able to spend a large portion of my pay on clothes as I needed the money; of course, I'd end up buying a few new clothes every now and then. Luckily, I was stocked up on professional clothes from my banking days and styles hadn't changed much.

The owner of the store took a special interest in me; I was told by one of the salesmen he took a special interest in all new managers. I played dumb as I knew what the salesman meant and I didn't want to open a can of worms. It didn't take me long to see for myself; I was asked many times to stay late and try on new clothes so the owner could see how they looked on something other than a mannequin, me being that something. Every time I turned around there'd be recurring innuendos; not from the salesmen, but from the owner. I realized in order to keep my position I had to continually play his cat and mouse game; I was sharp enough to stay in the game without compromising a thing. I definitely knew I wouldn't be coming out to anyone at work; if the owner ever caught wind of it, I'd be extremely vulnerable.

It finally got to the point where I couldn't perform my job because of all the interruptions and special favor requests by the owner. I talked with him one day about the entire situation and at that point realized if I didn't give in to his propositions, I wouldn't be able to remain on as manager. I couldn't go to the police as it was rumored he had no problem giving certain individuals on the force free clothing in return for favors; I didn't want to become an enemy of the force. I thought about reporting him to the department of labor; however, he had a wife and children and I didn't really desire to be the cause of a possible family breakup.

After several months of putting up with the continual harassment and humiliation, I resigned my position. Whether the owner knew of my homosexuality, I can't say for sure; however, I do know whatever his reasoning was for his behavior, it cost me my job. That was my own first personal exposure to sexual or gay discrimination in the workplace, it wouldn't be my last.

COMING OUT

Throughout my employment at the clothing store, my wife and I worked on finalizing our divorce. It took some time, but we eventually agreed and sometimes agreed to disagree on all the details. It was eventually final and I was a single gay man!

Shortly thereafter I finally landed a position in my chosen field and could put that entire previous employment fiasco behind me. I realized I needed to diligently work at keeping my homosexuality a secret in the workplace; something I thought I'd done at the clothing store.

Coming out proved to be a continual never ending process and to this day still is; there'll always be someone or someplace where the issue of coming out will present itself.

7

Gay Dating

I didn't like living alone; I'd either lived at home with my parents or lived with my wife and sons, except for that attempt at my first gay relationship. I realized after that first attempt, I'd get to know someone a little more before inviting them to share my living quarters, even though living alone was for the birds.

I continued to attend meetings in the gay community whenever I knew about them; it got old after some time as it was always the same people in attendance meeting after meeting. I was becoming a regular, a regular stick in the mud and that definitely didn't fit my personality. Finally one of my friends I'd met earlier suggested we go out and play some pool at one of the gay bars in town. We'd go two or three times a week and I really enjoyed myself. I met several new friends and even dated some.

Gay dating was and still is definitely different than

straight dating in many ways. The majority of the guys I met only wanted one thing; they didn't care to go slow and get to know a person first, many times they didn't even ask your name. It appeared their idea of getting to know someone was having a few drinks and a dance or two at the club. Sounds a lot like straight dating for many of you I'm sure. Yes, there're many similarities, but one has to understand the many differences that exist. Many socially acceptable manners I was accustomed to in straight dating aren't openly available for gay dating; society won't allow it in most places.

One evening early on in my clubbing days I was approached by a guy at the bar, he introduced himself and asked if I'd like to watch a movie with him. He was well groomed appearing to have it together, I asked him what movie he had in mind and told him Saturday evening would be good for me; naturally, I thought he meant a movie at a movie theater. He said we didn't have to wait for Saturday and asked if I'd seen *Village of the Rammed*. I'd never heard of it nor did I ever see any advertisements for it; he said he thought it was the original and not any remake. I decided to go for it and he wanted me to ride with him, I told him I'd rather follow. We got in our cars and I followed; he eventually pulled in the driveway of a house and I thought maybe he just needed to pick something up, so I waited in my car leaving it running. He walked up to my car window and asked if I was coming in, I told him I'd just wait in my car. He started to laugh and couldn't stop so I asked him what was wrong. He asked how long I'd been out and I told him not that long. I ended up going inside with him and we had the best evening. He was a super nice guy; we never got around to watching the movie. To this day I haven't seen *Village of the Rammed*, have you? Wow, I still had a lot to learn about gay dating!

I continued to date occasionally. I eventually decided to take country and western dance lessons at one of the gay bars because many of the good looking nice guys you'd see around were cowboys; at least they wanted you to think they were. I went to the lessons with a couple friends; we'd stumble around and make fools of ourselves, but we finally picked up the country two step. We spent more time at the country bars than we did the others. I even went out and bought a black felt cowboy hat, along with some calfskin cowboy boots. I was ready to stomp butt on the dance floor and stomp butt I did, my own; my new cowboy boots were so slick on the bottom, the first night I wore them I fell flat on my butt the moment I hit the dance floor.

The hat and boots paid off. I met a local guy at a country bar and we seemed to hit it off. We started to date and appeared headed toward a nurturing and healthy relationship, or so I thought at the time. Little did I know I'd be trapped in a sixteen month relationship that would prove to be one of the most degrading and humiliating experiences in my life; going into all the details would be another book in itself.

LIVING THE DIFFERENCE

I was warned up front by a good friend of mine that I shouldn't get involved; I didn't listen. Everything seemed right at the onset. He was good looking, appeared educated, and seemed to have a level head on his shoulders; however, those attributes proved not only to be extremely misleading, but the total extent of any seemingly positive attributes he'd possess. The poured on charm disguised his true inner self. He was the axis upon which everything revolved around, or so he thought. Nothing could be what it actually was, it had to be what he perceived and wanted it to be, regardless of the truth. He could sway anyone his way no matter what the circumstances were. I learned the hard way I had to experience it myself.

By the time I gained back enough of my self esteem to get out of the relationship, a lot of damage had occurred. I ended up in therapy for several sessions before I overcame and reversed the damage the relationship had done to me. I didn't go out for some time. I was failing in my attempts at a gay relationship so I decided to throw myself into my new job.

I wore many hats in my new position. The company was a small door to door direct sales company headquartered in Oklahoma City with sales offices in several other cities. The owner was from the Eastern part of the country and had been in door to door direct sales for many years. I was in charge of the sales inventory, the accounting and financial data, the independent contractor sales force contracts, and whatever else the owner needed performed. It was a stretch to actually say the position was in my chosen field; it ended up being in many fields. I'm not complaining because jobs of any kind at that time were still few and far between in Oklahoma City; we were still recovering from the big oil bust.

The job somewhat resembled my old network marketing days, except I received a regular weekly paycheck with my new job. We'd have motivational meetings every morning to charge up the local sales force and occasional regional meetings for the entire sales force of the company. The job was good for me at the time. Many days I'd need as much motivating as the sales force; remember I was coming off two failed gay relationships.

I continued aggressively working my new position and became good friends with the owner, eventually becoming acquainted with certain members of his family when they were brought into the company during a period of rapid growth. I even put my oldest son to work; he became an independent contractor and earned his own money. He'd always shown a keen interest in the business sector and still does today.

During that time I'd become a member of the local gay Catholic church; I missed going out and meeting new people. I'd always attended church and thought by transferring to another congregation I'd be able to meet some nice Christian individuals from the gay community. I regularly attended the new church and met many new friends.

One such friend was a gentleman several years my senior. He'd just retired from a government job in another state and moved to Oklahoma City to be close to his family. He was quite the talker and had many interesting stories about his life experiences he wanted to share with me. We became close friends and began to see each other outside the church. I didn't consider us dating, just becoming close dear friends. He'd cook evenings and have me over to share a meal on my way home from the office. He'd recently lost his lifetime partner and was very lonely and starving for company in a new city.

We enjoyed going to the symphony, as well as dining out together. The movie *Pretty Woman* was released on video and he purchased a copy so we could watch it together. It became somewhat of a ritual with us and most Saturday evenings he'd cook while we watched *Pretty Woman*. One weekend I invited him to go to the local amusement park with me and my sons; everyone had the best time. I believe my sons thought at the time they were gaining another grandpa.

I thoroughly enjoyed the time we spent together; however, I could sense he wanted more. I never thought of him in that way and hoped what we had could continue on. One evening we went for a long walk in the park and he told me he was falling in love with me. I told him I had a sincere love for him, but I wasn't in love with him. He said he couldn't help his feelings and if I couldn't get to that same point with him, he wanted to end our friendship. I was devastated. I thought our friendship would last forever and could withstand anything; I was wrong. It'd be several months before I'd ever see him again.

FORCED ENDING OF A CLOSE DEAR FRIENDSHIP

LIVING THE DIFFERENCE

The direct sales business was continuing to grow and I decided whenever I could find some spare time I'd start going out again certain evenings on my way home from the office.

One evening after work I went to play pool with some friends. I went up to the bar to get a drink and there was a guy sitting at the end of the bar; he looked very familiar to me. I invited him to join us at the pool table and he did. We started talking and I asked where he was from. I knew it, I knew it, he was from Guymon, Oklahoma; we went to high school together. We didn't graduate the same year as he was a year or two behind me. He was coming off a divorce and it was the first time he'd been in a gay bar. I thought to myself, "I could teach him a thing or two!" Look at me, a seasoned homosexual. He finally recognized who I was; I had changed a lot since my high school years, I was working out and wasn't the skinny guy I was back then. We had a nice chat that evening and decided to go to dinner the coming weekend.

The weekend came and we went to dinner in *Bricktown*, a revived old commercial district just east of downtown Oklahoma City; it was Oklahoma City's first wholesale commercial district. The area was becoming the hot spot in the city for dining and was growing rapidly in the number of dining establishments and small businesses. We had a nice meal and decided to take in a movie afterward. We saw *Sister Act* and died laughing the entire movie.

GAY DATING

We dated a few times, but nothing real serious resulted. He hadn't come out to anyone, including himself. He was really confused and reminded me of someone not that long before. I tried to help him understand his feelings, but he wasn't ready and couldn't even be true to himself at that point; he was going to have a long difficult road ahead of him. I gave him the name of the psychiatrist I went to in hopes he'd be able to assist in his understanding and acceptance of homosexuality. We crossed paths a couple more times after that and he'd yet to accept who he really was.

I was meeting some very nice people both at church and at the clubs. One Saturday evening the church had a bingo night with a pot luck dinner. Everyone enjoyed the evening and a few of us decided to go to one of the clubs afterward. There were probably a half dozen of us going to the club and when we arrived the DJ was playing a medley of old disco songs. Of course the music put us in a partying mood and everyone went out on the dance floor; I'm sure we made fools of ourselves, but we were the happiest darn fools around. Most of the group finally left, a couple of us remained and sat in one of the booths talking the night away. On my way to the restroom, a guy came up to me and asked if he might join us at our booth; naturally I told him yes. When I returned from the restroom he was sitting on my side so I scooted right in beside him. Eventually the other guy from church left and it was just the two of us.

LIVING THE DIFFERENCE

We closed the bar down and ended up at Denney's for an early morning breakfast. We really had a lot in common; he also had a degree in accounting and previously worked in an oil related industry. We finished our breakfast and continued talking for over an hour. He finally asked if I'd like to go out with him that Sunday evening; he said there was a *drag show* at one of the clubs and he'd just meet me there. I'd been to a couple *drag shows* and they were very entertaining, I told him I'd see him later that evening.

I arrived a little early to the show and sat down at a table close to the stage. I ordered a Coors light and waited for him to show. I waited and waited and waited and he never showed. The show was about to begin so I decided to stay and enjoy myself. Just a short time into the show, one of the entertainers kept singling me out and tried to get me up on the stage; I hadn't a clue why. Then all of a sudden the entertainer started lip syncing the song *Getting to Know You*, I looked closely into the *drag queen's* eyes and realized it was my date from Denney's. He never mentioned a word to me about being a *drag queen*; I had no idea. After his performance he came over and sat down at my table. He apologized; he said if he'd told me at Denney's he was a *drag queen*, I probably wouldn't have accepted the date. He was right. I had nothing at all against *drag queens* I just wasn't planning on dating any. We both had a good laugh. I never went out with him again, but I did see him perform at a holiday charity benefit a few weeks later.

GAY DATING

Wow, I was really striking out in the dating arena. It was getting close to the holiday season and it looked like I'd be spending the romance part of it alone. I was fine with that as I had my sons and we always enjoyed the holiday season together. Of course they'd spend it at their mothers since we were divorced, but I still managed quality time with them during the holidays to exchange gifts.

The holiday season was an extremely busy time at the office and I didn't have time to go out much. Between working and gift shopping for family and friends, I'd very little time for anything else. One Wednesday evening I was able to squeeze in stopping at one of the clubs on my way home from the office to relax; I'm glad I did as it changed my life forever.

I ran into a guy that evening I'd seen a few times at the club and we always greeted each other in a rather unusual manner. We'd say hi by taking our index finger and swiping it back and forth against the others shoulder. Strange or omen, that evening would be no different. We talked a little before I decided to leave; I left early because I needed to get a good night sleep before a busy day scheduled the next morning at the office.

IT JUST FELT RIGHT

GAY DATING

The following Saturday evening I went out with some friends and ran into that same guy from earlier in the week; we did our normal greeting and ended up buying each other a couple beers. I drank Coors light and he drank Bud light; not that it mattered at the time, but eventually he'd convert me to Bud light. We kind of hit it off that evening and left the bar together. We decided to meet each other the next evening so we could talk more and get to know each other a little better. He was recently divorced and had a very young son. He hadn't come out to his entire family, but he knew he was definitely gay.

We started to date on a regular basis and enjoyed the time together immensely. He eventually came out to everyone in his family and I was finally able to meet them. His birthday was a short time into our dating so I took him to dinner at Red Lobster to celebrate; my birthday followed in a couple weeks and we continued the celebration. After a few dates we took in a country and western concert with some friends and it seemed we'd known each other forever.

We eventually met each others children and appeared well on our way to forming a lasting relationship. We also introduced many of our own friends to each other prior to that first Christmas. Christmas rolled around with the fun continuing with gift exchanges and our first Christmas party. When New Year's Eve arrived, we went to dinner and ended up spending a quiet evening at my apartment afterward. At that point, he hadn't met my family other than for my sons. It'd be some time before we'd make it out to Guymon, Oklahoma to meet everyone.

Many evenings we'd get together and eat pizza; little did we know at the time it'd become our signature dish. Sometimes we'd eat it out and other times we'd order in. For some strange reason each of us thought the other liked mushrooms on their pizza so we always ordered it with mushrooms. Finally, after choking down the mushrooms and seeing picked off mushrooms wilting in the empty pizza boxes the next day, we realized neither of us liked mushrooms. To this day we still joke about that!

We continued dating and finally realized it was becoming much more than that. In a few more weeks we decided to move his belongings to my apartment and begin our life together. Of course we had our ups and downs in the beginning as most couples do, but our caring for each other prevailed. During that time, we talked many times about looking for a house; we ultimately contacted a realtor and began our search.

We looked at several houses with our realtor and had a lot of fun doing it. Somewhere along the process we gave each other a verbal commitment of love. After several weeks of looking, we walked in a house and immediately knew we'd found the perfect house to make our home. We gave the realtor an offer and the sellers accepted it. It'd be some time before we'd be able to close on the property as I was going through an old mortgage banking buddy of mine for the loan and that process in itself would take several weeks. Home loan processing at that time wasn't the speedy process we know today.

I'd always heard that practice makes perfect; all my attempts and fiascos at gay dating finally appeared to have paid off.

8

Settling Into The
Right Relationship

The home loan was approved and we began packing for the move into our new home. I finally had the feeling I was settling into the right relationship. No one knows whether a relationship will turn out to be the right one in any society, gay or straight; one can only do what feels right and proceed ahead with determination, while maintaining a certain level of caution.

After a few delays the loan finally closed; we were ready to make the move. We borrowed a pickup and ended up making several trips; while the move was only from a two bedroom apartment, the apartment was jammed full of furnishings. Between the two of us, we managed to come up with ample furnishings for the twenty one hundred square foot two story home; eventually we purchased a few items to fill in the voids.

CLOSING AND MOVING DAY ON OUR FIRST HOME

SETTLING INTO THE RIGHT RELATIONSHIP

Within a couple days we brought our sons together to meet for the first time, we went to pick them up early on a Saturday morning and had them for the weekend. It was one big party that weekend. We gave the kids a large bedroom upstairs and let them loose. We ended up going to a movie that Saturday afternoon after extensive debate among the kids as to what movie they wanted to see. We went to eat pizza after the movie and all appeared to be going fine. On our way home, we stopped at a movie rental store and rented *The Goonies* to watch later that evening. Everyone had the best time and the kids got along fantastic.

Keep in mind neither of us had come out to our sons at the time; there were bound to be some unanswered questions in their minds. We'd set up the house to appear we each had our own bedroom and while our kids were there, we actually slept in separate bedrooms. That first night just before everyone was off to bed my oldest son pulled me aside and said, "Dad, why is he living here with you?" I was somewhat caught off guard, but managed the reply, "We are sharing the house because he just went through a divorce like I did earlier and he needs a place to live." I went on to say, "This helps me out too because it's expensive to live alone and he'll help buy the groceries and things like that." My son appeared satisfied for the time being. It wasn't long after and his son started to cry because he missed his mom. Before long all the kids were upset with one thing or another so we each took our own kids and let them sleep with each of us in our individual separate bedrooms. That first weekend of everyone being together was great it actually went off without a hitch.

The next several weeks allowed us to really become acquainted with each of our individual habits. By the time anyone reaches the ages we were at that time, one is somewhat set in their own ways. For us to adapt to those ways and work around and accept each of our individual habits, compromises came into play. I'm not going to say it was easy, but we each possessed the determination and desire to make it work. Living the life we were each born to live made it that much easier.

Easter Sunday was upon us and we were invited to his mothers for brunch. I was a little apprehensive because it'd be our first time to appear as a couple in front of his entire family, including his aunt and uncle. We arrived and there was a houseful of people; I was very nervous. As it turned out my nerves settled down immediately, his entire family appeared very accepting; his mom would eventually become another mother to me and his aunt and uncle would become extremely close.

A few weeks after that we took our first trip together; we flew to Las Vegas for a few days. It was a last minute trip and we only found rooms available in downtown Las Vegas, not on the strip. We still had a great time, just spent a little more on cab fare than we anticipated; we more than made up for it with the inexpensive food available in all the casinos. One thing we definitely noticed about

SETTLING INTO THE RIGHT RELATIONSHIP

Las Vegas was virtually anything and everything was allowed there. Both of us had been there before, but with our wives at the time. On our trip together, we felt totally comfortable being there as a couple and walking down the street together as two gay men; we even gave each other hugs whenever we'd hit a jackpot playing the slot machines. It was a far cry from the atmosphere around Oklahoma.

Time went on that first year and between our jobs, children, and new home, we stayed extremely busy. Summer arrived and we worked extensively in the yard. Before long fall was upon us and we decided to take a trip back east in time to view the beautiful fall foliage.

My significant other had yet to meet my family so we decided prior to the trip back east, we'd head out to the panhandle of Oklahoma to pay them a visit. Of course my mom, being the cook she was, had a table full of food and desserts waiting for us when we walked through the door; she had my dad run to the store the minute they knew we were coming so she'd have my favorite dishes prepared. My sister came by for lunch that day and we sat down to our first meal together as a new family. He fit right in. We stayed and visited for an hour or two after lunch before proceeding on our trip back east; we backtracked a little with our trip to the panhandle, but it was well worth the diversion.

We had a fantastic trip back east. On the way, we stopped in Memphis and tried to spot Elvis, no such luck. We took the back roads whenever we could and saw some beautiful scenery. We stopped in Virginia to visit my brother and his wife and truly enjoyed the visit, it was his first time to meet them; unbeknownst to either of us at that time, we'd become best of family and friends treasuring their love immensely. We continued on to Washington, D.C. to see the sights and then began our return trip taking an entirely different route back to Oklahoma. We literally drove the wheels off and wore the brakes out on my Audi, but did make it home it one piece.

Another instance eventually came up with the kids that posed a challenge to us early on and that time it was his son who saw something when he was spending a couple weeknights with us. Early one morning before his dad took him to pre-school, he woke me up to give me a kiss goodbye, neither of us saw his son in the hallway, but he saw us. His son wanted to know why we kissed each other, we could tell it really bothered him. We were at a loss for words. The only thing we could come up with to tell him was his dad had something in his eye and I was looking very close at it to find the object and remove it. It was pretty iffy as to his buying the story at the time; all we could do was hope and let time tell. We really had to be careful around the kids and at times it was difficult to catch ourselves in time.

Throughout that first year we managed to maintain our sanity while learning a lot about and from each other. Every day was a learning experience. It was to the point of having many more ups and very few downs. Pretty good for a real *h-o-m-o-s-e-x-u-a-l* relationship!

In the meantime, I kept very busy at the office, it was a revolving door. As soon as any of the independent contractors would leave, we'd bring in that many more as it was door to door direct sales, the more contractors the more sales. One day I was going over the contract with one of the new contractors and she point blank asked me if I was straight or gay. I was stunned and my immediate response was, "Why, you want to start dating?" I went on to say, "It's against company policy to date contractors." She never questioned me again. I was an old pro with any questions or comments thrown my way or at least I thought so at the time.

We divided our time during the holidays between our two families. Our sons were also shuttled back and forth during the holiday season. There were plenty of families for everyone and the kids actually came out of the holidays with more gifts.

Before we knew it the first of the year was upon us. My sister telephoned asking if I knew my niece, the youngest daughter of my other sister, was engaged and planning to be married soon. I told her I hadn't heard the news. She asked if we'd like to rent a van in Oklahoma City to drive up to the panhandle and pick her up, along with mom and dad; we'd all travel together back to South Dakota in one vehicle for the wedding. I told her it was a great idea; my significant other and I immediately turned in vacation requests.

LIVING THE DIFFERENCE

In a few days my sister telephoned again telling me my other sister would be calling any day and I needed to be prepared for her asking me to come alone or not at all; she went further in adding the comment, "You know how she can be, we all do!" I couldn't believe my ears. Sure enough a couple days later my other sister telephoned and said, "J.C., I have to put my foot down, I really don't want both you and your significant other at the wedding, if you won't come alone, please don't come." I didn't know what to say. She went on and on trying to convince me it wasn't her and that it was the future mother in law she thought might have the problem. I knew better, I knew exactly who didn't want both of us there. I told her I'd let her know.

I had no intention of going after that, alone or with my significant other. Additionally, I wasn't planning on calling her back informing her of such. I immediately telephoned my other sister and told her what happened. She said there was an opportunity for her to go on a little vacation to Florida at the same time as the wedding and she'd rather do that anyway. Since my parents were of the age they didn't want to drive that far alone to the wedding, nobody from Oklahoma went. It's sad that such narrow mindedness caused the absence of so many people from the wedding. My parents were really hurt by the entire ordeal; they made a special effort to apologize to us on behalf of their daughter, my dear sister. It wouldn't be the last time they'd have to apologize on her behalf.

I never thought I'd see such narrow mindedness from

anyone in my family, I was wrong; it'd happen again down the road and include another member of my family as well. I guess I was still naïve as to the total understanding and acceptance by others; in my mind, it was very straight forward, there was no margin of error for interpretation, you are what you are and it is what it is. That sounded a little narrow minded didn't it? Oh well, what can I say, it's hard being gay; I've never said it was easy!

The new year continued and one day at the office the sales manager was celebrating her birthday. All the sales contractors went together and hired a male dancer to surprise her. I'd been gone the previous day and didn't know of their plans. There was a large separate meeting room in the back of the office where the sales meetings were held; the sales manager and her contractors were in the middle of their daily sales meeting when I arrived to work that day. I went in my office and sat down at the desk. In a couple minutes the front door buzzer went off and I went out to see who was there. It was a guy dressed in a police uniform, but I could tell it wasn't genuine. I took a closer look at his face realizing it was someone I went out with not long after I came out and started dating. I couldn't think of his name, but he definitely recognized me; he said, "I guess I'm here for you, it must be your birthday!" Before I could say anything he turned on some music and began to strip. The door flung open from the meeting room and everyone ran into the reception area. I still didn't know about the plan to surprise the sales manager and could only assume someone was playing a joke on me; it wasn't that unusual for joke playing at the office. Finally, one of the contractors yelled at the stripper and told him he was supposed to bust into the meeting room performing his routine for the sales manager. Thankfully the stripper and I realized what happened and went along with the crowd.

On my earlier date with him, I hadn't a clue he was a stripper and maybe he wasn't at that time, I never asked. To this day I don't know if anyone from the office ever put two and two together; they'd eventually learn of my homosexuality, but I don't believe the stripper incident lead them to that conclusion. I never told my significant other about that day. Going home and telling him someone I dated a couple years ago, before I met him, came by the office to strip for me just didn't seem like the thing to do. I wasn't trying to keep anything from him I was just protecting our relationship from something that could've become an unjust and unwarranted issue.

Having been together a little over a year at the time, we were still speaking to and living with each other; for many gay couples, feats in themselves. I guess our relationship was more than just average, it was very special. We decided we needed to celebrate so we took a trip to Hawaii. It was our way of kicking any down times we had early on in our relationship right out the window to the ocean below, while flying high celebrating our future together. It was an extremely long flight; neither of us had been on an airplane for that length of time.

We had the time of our lives, it was our delayed honeymoon. We sent postcards back home to everyone and managed gifts for them as well. We stayed ten days on Waikiki beach and enjoyed every last second of our time there together.

It finally came time to get back to reality. We arrived home and it was back to the grindstone. While gone, we missed our sons tremendously and decided then we'd have to plan out next big vacation with the kids in mind taking them with us.

Time continued on and during the first few years of our relationship, I always took a flower arrangement, special centerpiece for the dining room table, or a special garden treasure home with me every Friday for the weekend. Not only would it be something for my significant other to look forward to every week, but it'd signify something special we had together. It'd also introduce me to someone very special, someone who'd become a good friend for life.

The good friend being a nice individual I met at the flower shop just down the street from my office at the time. She'd never disappoint me with what she'd come up with; all I'd do was give her a call or stop by the shop and she knew exactly what to do for that special something for the weekend. We became close friends eventually meeting each of our individual families. There was positively a special aura about her that drew people in; she was a very sweet lady and still is today. My significant other and I felt extremely comfortable whenever we were in her presence or the presence of anyone from her family; to this day, we treasure their friendship immensely. It was a great feeling at the time to know our gay relationship wasn't given a second thought in the minds of our new friends.

In the meantime, my significant other and my ex-wife had become friends, they appeared to hit it off from the start; it was a blessing to me and my sons. I wish the same could've been said at the time about his ex-wife and me. I tried from the very beginning to be totally understanding of what she was going through, but nothing I'd say or do was right or good enough. It went from her ignoring me totally whenever I was in her presence to saying derogatory comments behind my back. Eventually, I'd avoid contact altogether for the sake of everyone, even though I wanted so desperately to get along for the benefit of my significant other and his son.

After a few years when she finally realized I didn't pose a threat to either her or her son, we were able to be in the same room without much difficulty. We still don't enjoy the kind of friendship that exists between my significant other and my ex-wife; maybe some day that can be there. It has to be extremely difficult for any woman to understand and accept when their husband comes out wanting a divorce; I can't even begin to imagine what that feeling must be like.

SETTLING INTO THE RIGHT RELATIONSHIP

As far as our sons, I can say without a doubt in my mind, it wasn't that far in our relationship when they considered each of us like their own second dad. The closeness we all shared early on continues to grow deeper and deeper each ensuing year.

The first tragedy in our relationship came with the death of my significant other's father. While they didn't have a very close relationship, I sensed his loss was deeper than he let on. With his mother and father being divorced many years prior, I never had the opportunity to meet his father.

It wasn't long after that first tragedy another tragedy occurred. That tragedy was extreme and outreaching affecting thousands of lives forever. It was the bombing of the *Alfred P. Murrah Federal Building* in Oklahoma City. It was a day that'd change the landscape of downtown Oklahoma City and the lives of thousands of Oklahomans forever. While our home at that time was several neighborhoods away, my significant other felt the blast as he was getting ready for work. His first thought was a severe earthquake had occurred, he remembers our entire home shaking. I was already at my office and remember hearing something that resembled a loud sonic boom.

We were immediately on the telephone with each other trying to figure out what happened; it'd be some time before reporters and newscasters would actually know what caused the blast. The following day when many of the details were released, the owner of the company talked with me about the possibility of doing something through the company to help raise money for the victims of the disaster and their families. Within a couple weeks, the company produced the *Oklahoma City Bombing Memorial Pin* and through sales and distribution of the pin, assisted in fundraising efforts for the victims and their families.

The bombing was devastating, everyone felt the resulting sorrow and deep hurt, even our young sons. After several months of assisting in the fundraising efforts, we decided it was a good time to take our sons away from the devastation and go someplace where they'd be able to focus their attention on some family fun and exploration. We went on our next big vacation and took the kids to Disney World.

When we told the kids about the upcoming vacation they were so excited it was all they'd talk about every time we saw them. It was finally time to leave. My sons had been on an airplane before, but they were too young to remember, so basically it was the first time for any of the kids to actually experience the thrill of flying. To see the expression on their faces when the airplane taxied down the runway and finally took off was priceless. The flight had a few bumps along the way, but the kids were determined not to look scared in front of their dads.

We arrived and took the shuttle bus to the theme park.

SETTLING INTO THE RIGHT RELATIONSHIP

We stayed at one of the park's hotels so we'd be right in the middle of the fun. We were all crammed into one room with two queen beds and a twin rollaway. Originally I'd planned to sleep on the rollaway, my sons planned to share a bed, and my significant other and his son planned to share the other bed. That's not the way it ended up. His son wanted a bed alone so he slept on the rollaway and my sons still wanted to sleep together so it left the two of us to sleep together in the other bed. At first we were reluctant to sleep together, but decided if we made a big deal out of the sleeping arrangements, it'd draw more attention to us than not; it really was a vacation for us after all!

If you've never been to Disney World, please go! Words can't describe the thrill and excitement of experiencing everything available to do at the park. It's more than a theme park it's a world totally separate from the everyday world we all live in. My significant other and I had just as much fun as our kids, actually more because we got to see our kids have the time of their lives.

TOGETHER AS A FAMILY AT DISNEYWORLD

SETTLING INTO THE RIGHT RELATIONSHIP

We weren't sad when the time came to leave. We'd seen and done so many things, there was still a lot of excitement inside us all; we'd live the experience for some time to come and still do today. It's the type of vacation that'll live on forever in our memories.

Everyone finally settled back to their regular routines. When I got back to the office, business had slowed down substantially. The owner was even talking about the possibility of closing the Oklahoma City office. It wasn't so much the slow down in business as we'd experienced that many times before and it'd always pick back up, it was the fact the owner looked to have virtually drained all the funds from his own company; the funds were just not there to pay the operating expenses. The owner had always taken care of writing the checks paying the operating expenses himself and I'd receive the check stubs and cancelled checks from him for recording purposes. Eventually, the check stubs and cancelled checks stopped coming and I started receiving telephone calls not only locally, but nationally from our other locations as well; nobody was getting paid. I hadn't a clue as to what the owner was up to or why the creditors were calling me.

I was finally able to uncover some past business practices of the owner and sure enough, not that he'd done anything illegal, but many of his past business ventures ended up the same way. He'd then go on to a new venture in new locations going through the cycle all over again, many times leaving someone behind to blame for his business failure and to clean up any resulting mess. I didn't want to be that person, but it was already too late.

Somewhere along the way, my homosexuality became known around the office; it didn't seem to matter at the time. What did matter were those telephone calls I'd started to receive from our many creditors; one such call ended with the creditor saying, "Do you know who the *faggot* is that ran the business into the ground, I heard the owner had a gay office manager who wasn't paying the bills?" I received numerous telephone calls before the office finally closed with the majority of them containing a mention of a homosexual employee running the business into the ground. I was already that scapegoat. I didn't even bother to explain to the creditors what the owner had done at that time and many times prior; it was quite obvious someone had already circulated false stories as to the business demise. I was even threatened by one of the local creditors who'd done some work for the owner and knew I was the office manager; he said, "You'd better come up with the money the owner owes me because you're the office manager and I hold you responsible you frickin' *faggot*."

The day I resigned my position at the company to the owner via fax, as well as verbally over the telephone, he told me he was on his way to Oklahoma City and wanted me to wait for him. That was around nine in the morning and he mentioned he was only a two hour drive away. I wrapped up what I could and was ready to leave by noon.

SETTLING INTO THE RIGHT RELATIONSHIP

I telephoned the owner a second time and he told me he was almost there. I waited for over three more hours and he never showed. I finally left around four in the afternoon leaving a long note for him explaining where things were at, and after locking the office door, slid my key under the door.

Around five that afternoon the owner showed up at my personal residence and I wasn't there; my significant other was home and he telephoned me on my cell telling me the owner was at the front door lashing out all kind of threats against the two of us and our families. The owner was known for idle threats in order to get his way by scaring people, so I told my significant other not to let him in and tell him I'd call him in a couple days after he cooled down. He finally left. I talked with the owner later that evening as when I arrived home and my significant other told me some of the threats, I wanted to nip it in the bud immediately. The owner was upset I didn't wait for him and I told him for all I knew I could've been waiting for days; there were many times the owner would say he'd be in the Oklahoma City office at a certain time and never show.

Many of the threats related to our homosexuality. They were hard for both of us to take. It's hard to imagine someone would resort to such tactics for personal satisfaction. I'd always known discrimination was everywhere I'd just never experienced it personally as much as I did during such a short period of time in my life.

LIVING THE DIFFERENCE

There I was unemployed again. My significant other and I had talked in the past about someday starting a business together so I visited with him again in more detail about the subject. We discussed it several times before we decided to give it a try. We decided to open somewhat the same type of business I'd been employed in for the past several years, except our door to door direct sales business was going to include a diverse product line.

We came up with a business idea and immediately began work on the plan. It'd be several weeks before we'd be ready to open the doors to our new business. In the meantime, my significant other resigned from his job and we were ready to embark on our first business venture together. The doors opened and our new business was called IMC (International Marketing Concepts). It'd be a true test of our relationship as not only did we live together, but we'd be working together as well. After a few weeks of being open, we held an open house for the business; friends, families, sales contractors, and many others joined in the festivities.

Before we knew it, the first anniversary of the Oklahoma City Bombing was upon us. We came out with the *Oklahoma City Bombing Anniversary Bible Necklace* to continue the fundraising efforts for the victims and their families. There was still a lot of pain and suffering from the bombing at that time and we wanted to do what we could to assist in alleviating some of it.

It wasn't too many months after that we decided to

reorganize the business and possibly expand to another state. The Oklahoma City market for door to door direct sales had shown a few signs of regression as in the past and while it'd always bounce back, we wanted to take a fresh look at a new market. We turned the local business over to one of the sales contractors and put our home up for sale beginning preparations for a move to Colorado. The thoughts in the back of our minds at that time were such that if the Colorado market proved rewarding, once the business was established, we'd come back to Oklahoma. It was going to be difficult leaving the kids for a time, but we knew we'd fly them out to visit and be back ourselves for visits.

By that time, I knew I'd settled into the right relationship.

9

Admitting A Wrong Decision, Going Forward

The move to Colorado proved to be a wrong decision for many reasons. First of all, we missed our kids tremendously even though we flew them out for a vacation and drove back a couple times to visit them. Secondly, Colorado Springs was an extremely difficult place to fit in and meet people. We weren't there long enough to figure out if the misfit was due to our homosexuality or because we were outsiders from Oklahoma; either way, we didn't feel comfortable in Colorado Springs. The climate didn't agree with me and I experienced many health concerns during our brief stay. Last and by no means least, the business climate in Colorado Springs wasn't conducive for a door to door direct sales business. Luckily we didn't buy and only rented while we were there.

When we telephoned our kids and told them we'd be moving back to Oklahoma in the near future they were ecstatic. They immediately asked when and my youngest son told me he wanted to come up to help us pack. I told him that wasn't possible because he'd have to miss too much school; he was ok with that but said, "Please hurry dad-e-o!"

We looked at the brief stay as somewhat of an extended vacation. We drove all around the mountains and visited the majority of the tourist attractions throughout the state. One thing we've always associated with our time in Colorado was the death of *Princess Diana, Lady Diana Spencer Princess of Wales.* Her death coincided with a weekend trip we took through the mountains; ironically, it was the last trip we'd take through the mountains prior to our move back to Oklahoma City.

We did leave our mark in Colorado Springs though. One day while taking an early evening walk, we came upon a new development of residential homes. We went inside some of the partially constructed homes and on the outside of one the curbing leading to the driveway had just been poured; we each found a stick and began to carve our initials in the cement. We've often thought about taking a vacation to Colorado Springs and going back to that neighborhood to see if our initials would still be there.

In the meantime, we were in Oklahoma City a few weeks before the move back looking at houses. We'd driven around various neighborhoods and came upon a house that caught our interest from the exterior so we called the realtor on the sign. The realtor met us there within the hour;

she was an elderly woman and immediately asked who the interested party was. She went on to ask if either of us were married and had any children. When we told her it'd be the two of us and every other weekend our children would be with us, she immediately informed us there was a contract on the house. We asked if there were others she could show us and her reply was she didn't really have many listings at that time; it was quite obvious she didn't want to show us houses. My immediate response was, "You are able to show us any realtor's listing aren't you?" At that point, she told us she was late for an appointment and drove off in her car. We both looked at each other and said a few choice words in our description of her character.

The next day we continued with our search. We weren't getting anywhere so we looked in the yellow pages and picked a realtor at random to call. It was another woman; we told her our price range, the type of houses we were interested in, and the neighborhoods that'd work. We also told her about our experience the previous day and told her if she was homophobic in any way just to hang up the telephone. She stayed on the line telling us to give her a couple hours and she'd call us back with some houses to show, along with a place to meet. It was less than two hours when she called back and gave us an address to meet her at. She was extremely nice and eventually showed us the house that'd become our second home together.

We went back to Colorado and began packing. We were so excited to be moving back to Oklahoma we couldn't wait. Within a few weeks we were on our way home. It was a long trip back, along the way we stopped and spent a couple days with my parents. We eventually arrived in Oklahoma City on a Saturday and had until Monday to turn in the moving truck we'd rented; it became an extremely busy weekend.

Our new home was in a historic neighborhood and had many dated characteristics and features. We decided to leave many of the original aspects of the property alone to preserve the history and charm of the house. We eventually updated a few of the features to bring that charm into the present period styles of the time. Our kids loved the house, mainly because of two flights of stairs for them to run up and down and a huge den in the back to lounge out in and watch television; it was home again and our kids were a part of it.

The business climate for door to door direct sales had pretty much dried up everywhere by that time, including Oklahoma. My significant other began working in the hospitality business and I began circulating my resume for a position in my chosen field again. I'd become proficient at sending out resumes by that time and probably topped the quantity I'd ever sent out for a single job search. Interviews were few and far between with no substantial offers the first several weeks.

During that time we cut back severely on our spending because with only one of us working at the time, we didn't want to skim too much off the savings. When the kids were over we'd rent movies rather than go to the movies and we'd cook at home instead of dining out. It was good experience for us; it taught us the concept of frugality.

With all my interim spare time, I managed to meet the majority of our new neighbors. We became known as the new gay couple on the block; there was already one gay couple who kept pretty much to themselves. A variety of professionals lived on the block ranging from an attorney, a plumber, to the minister right next door. Our next door neighbors were extremely nice; the fact of a gay couple living next door didn't seem to matter or bother them at all. They'd eventually move, but it was church related and had nothing to do with us; we ran into them a few times after their move and it was like old friends seeing each other. We felt very comfortable with our new surroundings.

I finally received a telephone call one day about a resume I'd sent to a group of private professionals. An interview was scheduled for the following day and after interviewing I felt confident I'd be offered the position. A couple days went by before I received a second telephone call, that time it was from the *top dog* of the company and I was drilled with several questions. I was told to sit still and I'd hear back shortly. A couple more days passed and no telephone call so I assumed they'd offered the position to someone else. The weekend was upon me and naturally I was on pins and needles the entire time.

LIVING THE DIFFERENCE

The following Monday morning I received yet another telephone call and was asked to come in for a second interview that afternoon. I went in and was finally offered the position; it was one of the most unusual interviewing processes I'd ever been through. I accepted the position with no knowledge at the time it'd end up being a position that'd almost end my life.

10

Position Of Persecution, Life Went On

My first day in my new position was very different. I was told immediately by the *top dog* it didn't matter that I reported to someone else, whenever I was told to do something from the *top dog's* office it needed to be done immediately. I was informed that office answered to no one but the owners of the business. I was also informed there were many varying personalities existing within the office, but it was the *top dog's* personality that mattered since that position ran everything for the owners. I was told I needed to keep everything within my own job responsibilities in an extremely organized manner, as well as any additional tasks I'd be given to perform. I was also told I was never to go to the owners about or with anything, if I did, it was grounds for dismissal. After about three hours of being lectured to, I was taken around the office and introduced to everyone.

I was finally left with the office manager, the one who initially interviewed me for the position. The office manager went on to tell me I'd be reporting to that position as the *top dog* had only been there a short time prior to my arrival; I was surprised at that information as hearing the *top dog* tell it, I'd assumed they'd both been there forever. I realized at that point there was a tremendous amount of animosity between the two of them.

BOSS FROM HELL WITH A BITE TOPPING ANY DOG'S BARK

LIVING THE DIFFERENCE

After just a few weeks, I realized I needed to kiss the *top dog's* ass continually, as well as stroke the ego daily or else I wouldn't survive. The *top dog* had known one of the owners for some time and appeared to be on a pedestal that'd never be toppled; that knowledge was well known throughout the company and used continually to enhance the performance of all employees. I knew I was very good at my profession and no one could take that away from me; I needed to prove that to the *top dog* in as short of time as possible in order to make everyday life at my new position bearable.

In the meantime, the kids were growing up. My oldest was about to turn sixteen and I'd promised my sons I'd buy their first vehicle when they obtained their driving license. Several weekends before his sixteenth birthday we started looking at cars. We looked and we looked coming across only pieces of junk in the price range we were trying to stay within. Every weekend the kids were at the house we'd go out looking at cars. It finally came to within just a few days of his birthday and no car. I took a couple days off and went on a thorough car search, finally finding two cars I wanted him to see; my significant other and I drove both cars over to his mom's house for him to take a look at. We finally found the car; his first car was a Saturn coupe.

Around that same time, my oldest son and I went for a long drive and I came out to him. Naturally he'd already figured out I was gay; that made for a much easier evening for me. We still talked about a lot of things that evening and it appeared I'd cleared up a lot of confusion surrounding certain instances or occurrences during the previous several years. We arrived back home and I felt we'd become closer than we already were.

At the time, I wished I'd recorded that conversation with my oldest son as I'd be having it again within a couple years with my youngest son. As it turned out, when I approached my youngest son a couple years down the road about having a talk, his reply was, "That's ok dad we don't need to do that." I could only assume he'd already figured it out and didn't need clarification on anything. At that point, I felt closer to him than I already was at the time. Chances were pretty high at that time my significant other's son would find out his dad was gay long before any talk between them could occur; with both my sons knowing and the kids around each other regularly, that conclusion was a no brainer.

Things at the office were continuing forward. By that time, my work load more than tripled and I'd been given an enormous amount of responsibility; the *top dog* kept dumping work on my desk, with much of it being from that office. The business was growing and more companies were being formed. Around that time, I received a salary adjustment; however, the amount was purely by accident. I'd been working an enormous amount of hours, weekends as well, and one day the *top dog* stopped by my office and told me a generous salary adjustment was turned over to payroll; it just so happened I was close friends with the payroll clerk, she'd already told me the day before a small adjustment was turned in and thought I'd want to know the exact amount before the *top dog* talked with me about it. The *top dog* hadn't a clue I knew the amount and in our conversation I mentioned what I felt I needed for a salary adjustment in light of all the added work and responsibilities; I was told it'd already been figured around that amount and was nice we both agreed, the *top dog* went on to say, "Don't worry J.C., I'll take care of you." The *top dog* immediately went down to payroll after leaving my office and changed the amount.

It was obvious at that time the *top dog* hadn't a clue I was gay. One day as I was walking by that office, I was stunned when asked if I'd heard about all the *dikes* working at one of the service companies we used. The conversation continued with the *top dog* slamming lesbians; I really wasn't that close to the *top dog* for that type of a conversation to occur nor did I feel it was appropriate. I guess the *top dog* thought it important my feeling somewhat of a closeness between us since I'd become such a valuable employee and the *top dog* didn't want anyone else or anything to interfere with my job performance or my happiness with the company. I was then told as I was leaving the office, "J.C., I felt very uncomfortable around those *dikes* when I was over there earlier this morning."

Well, work continued and the business continued to grow. I'd never worked so hard my entire life at any employment position. I'd finally accrued enough hours of work for some paid time off so my significant other and I drove down to San Antonio for a little vacation; I'd been there several years earlier and he never had so I thought it'd be exciting to show him around. It was a long drive down. We booked our stay at the *St. Anthony Hotel* just off the river walk; I'd stayed there during my earlier visit and remembered the charm of the aged and historic building that housed the hotel. We arrived, got all checked in, and headed down to the river walk. With both of us having recently worked an enormous amount of hours at our jobs, we decided not to plan a thing and just take it minute by minute.

The first evening we went inside what appeared to be a turn of the century pool hall and beer joint right off the river walk. We had a couple beers, of course Bud lights, and in a few minutes realized we were hungry from all the walking we'd done that afternoon. We looked around and noticed the establishment served pizza. We tried to find the server who'd brought us the beers earlier, but didn't see him so we signaled another server; we waited a few moments and signaled again, he never came over. In the meantime, we noticed other people getting served so my significant other went up to the bar and tried to order a pizza; he was told to sit down and someone would be with us soon. We waited and waited and no server. I mentioned to my significant other I thought we were being starred at so he looked around and thought the same. We decided to leave and as we got closer to the door noticed a small group of men following us. It didn't look good so we took off running out the door and down the street as fast as we could. We kept running and didn't look back; we finally got back to the river walk and mixed in with the crowd. We didn't know what was going on with those men and weren't going to wait around to find out.

The next day we were enjoying a margarita along the river walk and our waiter wasn't busy so we told him about the previous evening. He told us that particular place usually housed a rough crowd and it wasn't very gay friendly. I guess he assumed two men having a margarita together were gay because we never mentioned it to him. From that point forward we became more aware of our various surroundings.

We arrived back from our little get away and before long it was time to start the car search for my youngest son who was about to turn sixteen. We went through the same process on weekends, looked until we dropped. For some reason we lucked out that time, after just a couple weekends of looking we came across an older Ford Bronco that looked to be in excellent shape. It became his first car and he was very pleased. It'd be some time before my significant other's son would turn sixteen so we had somewhat of a temporary reprieve.

By that time, our comfort level with our neighborhood had dropped off drastically. The other gay couple down the block sold their house and moved out of the neighborhood; we ended up the only gay couple on the block. Shortly after that a house two houses down from ours sold and new neighbors moved in; immediately many of our other neighbors started to become less friendly toward us and we wondered what was going on.

One evening I was on the side of our house picking up some trash and heard our next door neighbor talking to the new neighbor; they couldn't see me so I perked up to hear what was being said. I couldn't make out the entire conversation, but at one point heard the new neighbor say, "How long have the two *fags* lived on the block?" Our next door neighbor said, "They've been here a couple years, but they've sure improved the looks of the neighborhood." His response made me feel as long as we served a purpose of improving the looks of the neighborhood it was ok for a gay couple to live on the block. He went on to say, "There was another gay couple across and down a bit and they finally moved." I went in the house and told my significant other about the conversation I'd just heard, he said it didn't surprise him; he told me he'd always felt our next door neighbor had a problem with us.

We tried not to let the situation bother us but it did. We finally asked the neighbor across the street what she'd heard; she was a single parent we trusted and had become close to. She told us the new neighbors were definitely homophobic and slamming us to the other neighbors. The thing that hurt was many of the existing neighbors were going right along with them. We weren't ready to make another move and still had improvements we'd started for the entire block that needed to be completed; they'd increase the property value for everyone. We decided to ride it out and see what happened.

I was still working a horrendous amount of hours at the office; of course being salaried, there was no extra compensation for all the overtime. Late one evening the *top dog* stopped by my office and asked what I thought about the new employee being tried out in the front office. I didn't know the employee and asked what the concern was. The next few words I heard floored me, "I'm sure he's gay and I don't know if he'll fit in." I immediately said if he did his job I was sure there'd be no problem.

The very next morning the *top dog* stopped at my office door telling me some drastic changes were about to take place and since we'd become so close, as long as I stuck around I'd be fine. I had no idea what that really meant, but I didn't have to wonder long. In a couple minutes the office manager I supposedly reported to stormed in my office throwing a bunch of invoices on my desk telling me to have fun, that position had just been eliminated. It wasn't long after the *top dog* came in my office and told me I'd be taking over many of the office manager's duties and responsibilities; it was also mentioned I'd probably be working late many evenings to get things straightened out.

It ended up I not only took over many of the office manager's responsibilities, but within a short time another person in management was fired and I was handed a few

of their responsibilities as well. I was literally working myself to death. I wouldn't get home in the evenings until
well after seven and I'd work most weekends; something
had to give. The *top dog* always told me I'd be taken care of
so I decided to give it some time and see what came up.

Down the road a ways, the *top dog* told me about the
possibility of the company hiring one of the *dikes* from
the service company we used and wanted my opinion.
I felt extremely uncomfortable hearing an individual referred to as a *dike*, but didn't feel comfortable telling that
to the *top dog* so I mentioned I'd dealt with the individual
under consideration a couple times over the telephone and
found her to be extremely competent and helpful in most
any area. I was then told she'd most likely be brought in
at a salary higher than mine, but not to worry as a special
compensation plan for me, in addition to my regular salary, was in the works. It was also mentioned the other
pay I'd receive occasionally from the owners for their own
personal work I'd perform wouldn't be changed.

Meanwhile, my significant other and I worked at com-
pleting the block projects in our neighborhood. We installed hanging planters along the wooded street sides and
were successful in declaring the block a historic site for
the neighborhood, with the appropriate signage at the entrance. We didn't know how much longer we'd be able to
weather the prevailing homophobic attitude existing on
the block and wanted to increase our own property value
prior to a possible sale.

LIVING THE DIFFERENCE

Back at the office, the *top dog* did hire and created a new management position for the individual from the service company. I was also assured that special compensation plan I'd been promised was definitely in the works. Business was still growing with location expansion plans nearing completion.

In the meantime, I was continually butting heads with the *top dog's* secretary; for some reason a feeling existed that my presence threatened that position. It came to be known the secretary felt threatened by many individuals, including the new manager recently hired; it wasn't long before the *top dog's* secretary was trying to pit me and the new manager against each other. It almost worked; thankfully the new manager and I ultimately became friends and realized what was going on.

The expansion was almost complete and the move into the new area was going to be extremely detailed and complicated; any hitch in the process could've disrupted the entire business operations. Throughout everything the *top dog* continually dumped more and more work on me; it was well known by that time, I'd always complete all the work no matter how much or how detailed it was.

One day the *top dog* finally woke up sensing I was about to jump ship from the amount of stress and the huge workload I was under; knowing that'd disrupt the plans for a smooth and orderly transition to the end, that special compensation plan that'd been talked about for so long finally became a reality. I didn't feel totally comfortable with the plan and the way it worked as the *top dog* had been known to have a reputation for deceit and certain mistruths. I documented many of our conversations with memorandums signed by both, with certain documentation being notarized by my own assistant at the time.

By that time, things were going downhill back at the neighborhood; many of the neighbors wouldn't even acknowledge our existence on the block. We decided to sell our house and move on some land somewhere in the country without any neighbors close by. We found a piece of land and went for it; it'd take some time before we'd be able to move as there wasn't a house on the property. That gave us plenty of time to sell our existing home.

In the meantime, the new manager hired from the service company eventually resigned her position; it appeared she'd had enough of the *top dog's* shenanigans. Who do you think some of her duties were dumped on? Of course, it was me. Many items remained to be completed resulting from the expansion and very few people left willing to do what it'd take to complete them.

I started to experience some health issues and after numerous tests were performed, it was determined I was suffering from certain stress induced conditions. I was put on medication and told to cut way back at the office; that was hard to do with everything going on at the time. The *top dog* told me to hire someone to help during that time, even if it'd end up being a temporary situation. I was finally given the go ahead to hire another individual so I took advantage of the opportunity and did just that; however, that gave the *top dog* an excuse to dump even more work on my desk.

I decided at that point I'd stay with the company seeing it through the complete expansion process and then find something with less stress involved. Little did I know at the time that was actually the *top dog's* intent, keeping me satisfied at the company throughout all the changes and expansion taking place; whenever that office would be able to get along without me, getting by with just the *top dog* and a family member, that'd be the end for me. I found out later, after my eventual departure, the *top dog's* plan all along was to bring a family member on board immediately after my time was up.

Throughout all that, my significant other and I sold our house and moved into a new house in the country. It'd be our third home together; wow, a possible record for a gay couple! At least the move alleviated the stressful situation we experienced in our old neighborhood with our homophobic neighbors. It also gave us space and privacy we'd not known up to that time. In time, we'd drive back to the old neighborhood and find it in total disarray. No one had cared for the block planters or the landscaping around the entrance sign. The houses looked run down and I imagined somewhat depreciated in value. It looked to us that it wasn't such a bad thing having a gay couple in the neighborhood after all.

Early one morning when I arrived at the office, my

assistant approached me about needing to borrow some money to help through a difficult rough time; I made the arrangements and lent the money. The next few days at the office proved very strange; a lot of small closed door meetings took place. The large weekly management meeting took place and it was rather unusual; while the *top dog* had no problem talking about others behind their back, it was never really done that much in the weekly management meeting, at least not in such an obvious manner. That day would be different, when the *top dog* was referring to one of the newer professionals in the group who had unexpectedly resigned the reference to him, as the one who went the other way and didn't like girls, was made. The *top dog* was extremely brazen that day and appeared somewhat intoxicated.

Later on in the day, I saw one of the other professionals in the group who I'd become good friends with and mentioned I probably wouldn't be there much longer, that my time was probably up; their response was, "Please don't leave!" While that response was nice to hear, it didn't change my thought process at all. Having been there around four years at the time and feeling my usefulness was nearly exhausted, as well as knowing how the *top dog* operated, I gathered up copies of memorandums and a few other items before I finally left for the day.

Sure enough, within the next few days I ended up tendering my resignation and all hell broke loose. During the process of finalizing certain aspects of my resignation,

I'd divulged certain facts about certain items to certain individuals; nothing I was barred from by any legal means. As a result, the next morning after my final day at the office, I received a death threat. I also received numerous telephone calls from friends at the office, as well as friends who'd either been terminated or resigned voluntarily during that time of expansion, turmoil, and unrest at the company. I was told to be prepared because the *top dog* was coming at me with both barrels loaded. As stated earlier, I'd divulged numerous facts and items to certain individuals the *top dog* definitely wanted to keep under wraps, including my special compensation plan which unbeknownst to me at the time it was agreed to and given to me, hadn't been divulged by the *top dog* to the owners of the business.

I realized at that point I was being targeted, but I also realized the many friends I had at the company who were coming to my rescue. I was told by the recently resigned manager at that time, the *top dog's* secretary mentioned in a meeting the *top dog* should just get rid of me, the *top dog's* reply was basically my work was too good and I was needed, also implying they'd have to find another way once my usefulness was exhausted; of course, I wasn't in that particular meeting. I was also told by another past employee the *top dog* had found out about my homosexuality and was definitely going to use it against me.

The supporting calls kept coming in, with one call from the spouse of the professional in the group I'd become good friends with, both of them working side by side; I was told they'd just resigned and wanted out of the company. When I asked why, I was told because I'd left and they didn't trust anyone left in management at the time.

That time in my life was very trying with numerous conversations and items of correspondence going back and forth between me and the company. Just when I didn't think it'd get any worse, I received a call one morning from an outside individual acting as agent for the company. I was told if I didn't get a cashier's check for an enormous sum of money to him in the next couple days for the company, they'd go to the police and have me arrested; he went on to inform me they'd say I stole my special compensation the *top dog* of the company paid me because the owners of the business weren't aware of the plan.

Something came over me, a feeling of helplessness; I was having a mental meltdown. My significant other drove me to a local hospital that afternoon and I was admitted. I was put in a ward with others experiencing severe mental meltdowns. It was a place I'd never known before; I was totally lost and at the mercy of the staff.

The first night in my new surroundings was very scary, patients were walking around mumbling and talking to themselves; some were trying to give others hugs and kisses, while some were even trying to take charge of the ward. I had to share a room with a young man who was schizophrenic; I was scared to fall asleep that first night.

During the night I woke up finding him in my bed and couldn't get him back in his own bed so I just slept the rest the night in his bed. When I woke up in the morning he was back in his bed with me.

I felt like a guinea pig, the doctors tried several different medications to help with my anxiety and depression. Nothing appeared to work; I'd cry at the drop of a hat. My significant other came by every day to visit me and my parents telephoned daily. My brother called several times, but I had a difficult time opening up to him, for no other reason than I was completely overwhelmed. One of the days my significant other was there he told me about a couple threatening telephone calls he'd received and thought it'd be a good idea if I engaged an attorney.

After a few days of getting settled in the ward and my meds adjusted, I engaged an attorney; after our initial consultation it was decided a proactive stance was the way to go and we filed a civil suit. Ample grounds existed for the action. Naturally a counter civil suit was filed in response.

I was finally released from the hospital and went home. The first several days were extremely difficult; I was terrified to stay alone when my significant other went to work for the day. Thank God I had my best buddy at my feet at all times, my dog Felix. Eventually I became less terrified and between meetings with my attorney, along with things at the house to do, I kept busy; we hadn't been at our new property very long and being on five acres there was a long list of items to get done at the time.

One evening my brother telephoned telling me he and his wife would be flying to Oklahoma City in a couple weeks and renting a car to drive out to the panhandle of Oklahoma to visit my parents. He asked if they could stay a few days at the house to spend some time with me and my significant other. I was very excited and told him that'd be fantastic. When they arrived we had a very nice visit; we didn't do much, just sat around, talked, and took some walks on the property. It was tough when they left and I was extremely sad for some time after they pulled out the gate.

Life went on and before long I was emotionally ready to begin another search for employment. I updated my resume and began my job search. I royally botched my first several interviews; I was constantly on the watch for indications anyone I'd interviewed with could possibly turn out to be like the *top dog* from my last position. After several failed attempts, I decided I needed more time before I went on another interview.

My significant other came home from work one evening and asked if I'd like to get away for a long weekend. That sure sounded good to me at the time and I thought just maybe it'd help get me back on track with my job hunting. A few days before we left my ex-wife called and asked if we'd like to give a home to a young puppy she'd recently found. Being the dog lovers we were, we told her yes. When we went over to pick the puppy up, all we saw was a small ball of fur; it was a young German Shepherd puppy. We left that following weekend for a small resort in Southeastern Oklahoma and took Felix and our new puppy with us. It was a much needed get away for both of us, we walked our dogs in the woods, relaxed, and cooked out a lot; we had a great time.

The next week I interviewed for a position in purchasing with a businessperson who'd become one of the most admired individuals I'd ever know. I immediately had a good feeling about their character the minute we sat down and started the interviewing process. I didn't give all the details about my horrific experience at my prior position, but in time I'd reveal the entire story. After interviewing for some time, I was turned over to the second in charge. A great person as well and I knew I'd found a home if they'd just hire me. In a few days I received a telephone call offering me the position and would start within a couple weeks. I was so thrilled to be among the working class again.

In the meantime, my sons were getting older. Since they had their own vehicles and were doing their own thing, we didn't see each other as often as we would've liked, but everyone understood. My significant other still had his son every other weekend and we enjoyed the times he was there.

Fourth of July was upon us, I really wanted to get everyone together and have a large cook out with a huge firework display. It took some doing, but it finally happened; over a dozen people showed up including our sons and some of their friends. Most of my sons' friends had known me a long time and they were cool with me and my significant other, the gourmet chef. The gourmet chef prepared the feast of all feasts that Fourth of July there was food and desserts to feed an army. Afterward, everyone had a fun time shooting off fireworks, with a gigantic firework display capping off the evening.

The legal civil suit was progressing; I hadn't a clue what I was in for. Things looked great with the suit, many individuals came forward on my behalf; it looked like I'd prevail in the long run. Throughout the process, my significant other was approached and offered a bribe to turn against me; of course, he refused and laughed at the attempt.

When needed, I had my new job to take my mind off the suit. My new position was totally different than anything I'd ever done; it was way off my chosen field. It was good for me as I didn't want any major responsibilities at that time, just a job with a paycheck and benefits.

It'd been some time since we'd seen my parents, so after a short time into my new job we took a long weekend and went out to the panhandle of Oklahoma to see them. My parents loved my significant other dearly and we always had the best time when we went home. That visit was extremely special as it was the first time I'd seen my parents since my meltdown. They were very supportive and it was a good wholesome family weekend.

LIVING THE DIFFERENCE

Many events in our lives occurred throughout those times. My youngest son starred in an independent film with the lead role as a gay teenager trying to grow up; he isn't gay by the way and if he were it'd be ok with me. Both my sons graduated from high school, with my oldest going on to college and my youngest moving out to Los Angeles to pursue his dream of an acting career. My significant other's son continued on with school and eventually turned sixteen; we gave him one of the family cars.

Then an unexpected turn of events occurred. I tried to take my life when I was informed the place I was previously employed by was trying to get criminal actions brought against me; having already been through so much, when I heard that news something inside snapped and I wasn't able to cope with life at the time. That was their way of making sure I'd drop my civil suit against them; they knew I couldn't properly defend myself in a criminal suit with a pending civil suit. With the way everything was going with the civil suit they stood to loose a lot when I'd eventually win that suit, which it appeared I would; in their minds I guess they'd no choice but to do what they did.

I woke up in a hospital intensive care unit very confused and disoriented. My significant other was standing at the foot of the hospital bed. He told me I'd taken a bottle of sleeping pills and he couldn't get me to wake up. I was transferred to another hospital and ended up in the same ward I was in at the time of my first mental meltdown. I spent several days in the hospital that time and upon release would continue on in therapy for a very long time.

I contacted several different defense attorneys and was amazed at the number who'd already either heard or read about the accusations. Many of them even attempted earlier contact with me, but were unsuccessful due to my stay in the hospital. As I was warned earlier by a friend and past employee of the same prior company, the issue of my homosexuality was definitely brought into it. I was even refused representation by a couple attorneys who didn't want to take a case involving a homosexual or someone in a gay relationship, I was outright told that; they even went so far as to say if I ever repeated that in any attempt of action, they'd deny it.

I eventually engaged one of the best defense attorneys in Oklahoma City to represent me, my new attorney had no problem whatsoever with my sexual preferences; I was in for a long grueling battle for the truth. One of the first items my new defense attorney needed from my civil attorney, in order for him to adequately protect me and proceed with my case, was for my civil attorney to arrange for both civil suits to be dropped; everyone mutually agreed and they finally got what they wanted.

During that time, another article appeared in the local newspaper detailing the criminal accusations. A few days later an individual who'd read the article sent a letter to my civil attorney detailing his own experience of an extortion attempt against him a few years earlier by one of the same

individuals. Between that, previous recordings on my behalf, various detailed documents on my behalf, and the
flat out truth, I felt when all the facts and circumstances
would be known, the truth would come out in the end;
I'd be vindicated. However, the system didn't work that
fast, that easily, or that straight forward, it'd be a long time
before all the facts and circumstances would be known,
if ever; it'd be an extremely long time before it'd all get
resolved.

No one could begin to imagine what it was like to hear
lies being spread about and appearing in large print in the
daily newspaper. You realize very fast who your real family and friends truly are. My own sister immediately telephoned my significant other. Rather than asking what she
could do for us, how I was doing, or even wanting to talk
with her own brother, she went behind my back and drilled
my significant other about the article; the local newspaper
was also distributed back in my hometown of Guymon,
Oklahoma. She demanded to know whether it was true
or not. Since her friends and neighbors back home would
realize she had a homosexual brother accused of wrongdoing, she was more concerned about any embarrassment
the article might cause her than about my own well being;
that truly hurt.

Certain family members from both sides of the family,
as well as certain friends, never did bother to call or even
broach the subject of my well being the next time I came
in contact with them. Were they too embarrassed by the

article? Was it just too much for them to associate with a homosexual accused of wrongdoing? Of course, I'd always been able to count on my significant other, my parents, my brother, my sons, my significant other's mother, his son, his aunt and uncle, certain friends, and even my ex-wife; they'd never disappointed me and gave their unconditional love and support at that time in my life as well. They'll never know how much it meant to me and how much I appreciated it. As far as the others, it was their choice to do or not to do something; it hurt, I didn't totally understand it, but I was able to accept it and go on.

I didn't know if I'd have a job to return to or not when I was released from the hospital. I was embarrassed myself to go back to work as I'd assumed many of the individuals I worked with had seen the detailed newspaper article. The first day I returned to work I was amazed, I was welcomed back with open arms from everyone, well almost everyone. I'd never known such an outpouring of love and support in the work place. I confided in certain individuals at work with enough of the details so they'd know the accusations were false, as well as extremely misleading.

11

Yet Another Battle

Between the continuances and the postponements, the legal battle would drag on for a few years. It was always in the back of my mind and was definitely a pull of energy from my body. I continually had meetings with my attorney, as well as numerous court appearances throughout the various stages of the judicial system. It was all I'd be able to do at times to drag myself out of bed and begin a new day.

I was fortunate to have a job to bury myself in. My employer was totally understanding of the time I needed off for the various reasons that existed at the time. My significant other was also totally understanding and supportive as well with everything disruptive going on in our own lives during that time.

It was around that same time I met someone; someone through one of the group therapy sessions I'd attended to help deal with my anxiety and depression. The individual was going through a rough stretch in his own life as well; he'd lost his job and his significant other. Some of us from that group would go for coffee at times, it was tremendous moral support; to my knowledge, the two of us were the only gay individuals in the group.

One evening after everyone left from coffee, the two of us remained. He asked how my significant other was handling everything at the time. I told him I was extremely fortunate to have someone as understanding and supportive as he was. I was about to continue on with my thoughts when he said, "Are you sure he's as understanding and supportive as you think, what's he doing this evening?" I really didn't know where he was going with that so I told him my significant other was probably at home watching television. He went on to say, "So you have total trust in him that he's home alone watching television, you should give him a call." By that time I was getting somewhat paranoid, all the anxiety and depression I was experiencing I'm sure helped that paranoia along. I took out my cell phone and called him; there was no answer. Immediately my heart skipped a couple beats as I was thinking the worse; mind you I hadn't a reason to think that, it was just the paranoia kicking in.

By that time any benefit I'd gained from the group session that afternoon was long gone. I felt terribly lost and alone; I didn't know what to do. He said, "Why don't you come home with me so you're not alone?" I told him I was just going to sit there, calm down, and then drive home, that I was sure my significant other would be there when I got home.

Sure enough, when I arrived home my significant other was in bed snoring and obviously hadn't heard the telephone ring earlier. I never told him what I went through that evening as he already had enough to deal with. What I did do was inform the group counselor about what happened and that individual was kicked out of the group for trying to take advantage of me with information he'd gained through the group sessions.

In the meantime, I just didn't feel good; I was always tired and worn out with no real drive within me. I assumed much of that was the anxiety and depression. One evening I passed out at home and ended up on the kitchen floor, I was in such pain I couldn't get up. My significant other called 911 and I was taken to the emergency room. The doctor determined the pain resulted from soft tissue damage; I was given a prescription for pain medication and sent home.

In the next few days the pain got worse and settled in my pelvic region. It felt somewhat like a pain I'd experienced years before when my sciatic nerve was irritated from an enlarged prostate due to an infection. I went to the first urologist who'd quickly work me in their schedule; after initial blood work and a precautionary set of prostate biopsies, it was determined I had prostate cancer. That determination was an accidental finding; I was only trying to get treatment for what I thought was something possibly causing sciatica. I actually did have sciatica, but it flared up from my passing out earlier in the kitchen and hurting my back, it wasn't from a prostate infection or prostate cancer.

God does work in mysterious ways at times; in all likelihood, it was the extreme stress I was under from everything going on at that time that caused me to pass out, which in turn eventually led me to the urologist who diagnosed my cancer. Prostate cancer is extremely difficult to accurately detect in the very early stages; many times it goes undetected for years and when finally detected, has spread to other areas. I was extremely fortunate everything occurred as it did.

I felt like a bomb was dropped on me when I heard the news. I didn't know how I'd be able to handle yet another battle put before me. I was alone when I received the telephone call from the urologist; I literally dropped the telephone receiver and feel to my knees. When I got back on the telephone, the doctor told me there were several treatment options, but I'd need to arrange for another doctor and my file would be forwarded; the urologist didn't want me as a patient. I thought that rather unusual and came to the conclusion it was because I was gay. On my first appointment, several questions were asked of me trying to figure out if I could've contracted a sexually transmitted disease causing an infection; all the answers I gave pointed to no. However, during that interview I was point blank asked by the urologist if I'd engaged in unprotected gay sex, not unprotected sex, but unprotected gay sex. The blood work proved no infection from any sexually transmitted disease; however, during the interview process the urologist found out I was gay.

My significant other was on a delivery for work and not reachable so I left a message for him. There I was home alone and told over the telephone I had cancer; the doctor didn't even want me as a patient, what more could've gone wrong, a lot! I needed someone to talk to so I telephoned my brother. He was very comforting and supportive, together we prayed to God. Before we ended our conversation I asked if he thought it'd be ok to tell our parents, I didn't want to upset them; my brother thought they needed to know. Before long my significant other called and I told him the news; he got all choked up and told me he'd be right home.

ANOTHER BATTLE BEGINS

In the meantime, I decided to call my parents. My mom answered and I asked her to have dad get on the extension; when they were both on I told them I had prostate cancer. They wanted to know how serious and if I'd be ok. I told them I'd just found out that afternoon and didn't have many details, but was sure everything would be ok. They told me my sister and her husband had arrived earlier in the day from South Dakota for a visit and was over at my other sister's house. My parents thought I should call over there and talk to them.

Being the homophobic individuals they were I was somewhat reluctant to even call and talk to my sisters. However, I really needed all the love and family support I could get at that time. I thought they'd definitely be supportive and comforting to a brother just diagnosed with cancer needing the love of his sisters. I made the call and I was wrong; I ended up talking with each of them individually and it was a huge mistake.

When my sister answered the telephone she was very distant, I told her the news and there was nothing coming from the other line, there was virtually no response at all other than some mumbling in the background; my feelings were extremely hurt so I asked her what was wrong and why she was being like that. Her response was, "Because you let dad help you out with some of your legal expenses." I couldn't believe what I was hearing and immediately said, "How can you be so cold, what does that have to do with what I'm trying to tell you now; besides, you know I needed more cash than I could come up with as fast as I needed in order to engage a good defense attorney, dad knows he'll be paid back real soon." I went on to remind her how many times our dad had to help her in the past. I couldn't believe I was having that conversation with her at that time.

Before I knew it, she'd handed the telephone to my other sister. The first words out of her mouth were, "What are you trying to pull here?" I was totally blown away with my sisters. Her next words were, "You probably don't even have cancer." Quite obviously the mumbling I heard earlier was my other sister telling her the news. I was about to hang up, but by that time I was getting angry; I said, "Do you even care if I live or die?" Her response was, "Right now I can't answer that." I hung up the telephone. For some reason something my sister said to my dad a few years prior to that time came into focus immediately after I hung up the telephone; on one of her visits home, she said to dad, "Why don't you just give us kids the majority of your money now while we're young enough to enjoy it." I remembered how surprised and somewhat hurt my dad had been with that comment; he told me and my brother about it soon after.

My significant other had walked in during the conversations and couldn't believe what he was witnessing. He was on the extension some of the time and heard the majority of the conversations with my sisters. He could tell I was fairly distraught and held me in his arms comforting and consoling me. I finally calmed down enough to eat a bite and then I went to bed.

The next morning was a Saturday and I was totally drained from the previous day. I decided to telephone my parents again and reassure them everything would be ok. I didn't want them to worry and had no idea what my sisters may have said to them. My sister's husband answered the telephone and wouldn't let me speak with my parents, he said, "I'm not going to let you speak with them because we're trying to have a nice weekend visit with them and they don't need to get upset about your cancer; you don't even know if you really have it or not, you're jumping to conclusions." He immediately hung up the telephone after he spoke. I knew in my heart it wasn't him talking, he was only voicing the thoughts of my sisters.

I needed to talk to someone in my family, if not for anything other than a few words of comfort. I telephoned my brother again and we talked for some time; I didn't mention to him at that time what happened with my sisters, I just wanted to hear his voice. He'd find out for himself what they did the next time he went to visit my parents.

That weekend seemed to last forever; I didn't think Monday morning would ever come around. I hadn't told my sons at that time as I wanted to go see another urologist and get a second opinion. When I arrived at the office that Monday, I told my employer and was told not to worry about whatever time I needed off. I immediately started calling various urologists trying to get in at the earliest possible time; I found one I could go see the next morning.

I went by and picked up my chart from the first urologist before my appointment. After the new urologist looked through everything, he immediately wanted to schedule surgery for a radical prostatectomy as soon as possible. My significant other was with me and we both became extremely concerned. The doctor didn't even want to perform his own set of biopsies; he did briefly review a couple treatment options, but stayed with his earlier suggestion of immediate surgery. He scheduled some additional scans for the next day to see if the cancer had spread; the scans indicated the cancer was confined to my prostate.

I decided I needed a third opinion prior to having such a severe life altering surgery. The third urologist performed his own biopsies and determined the cancer was minute enough to warrant a wait and see approach, putting off surgery until it was absolutely necessary. Prostate cancer normally has an extremely slow growth rate so at that time I decided to opt out of surgery. By opting out of surgery, I committed myself to prostate biopsies every few months to determine if the cancer was growing.

Prostate biopsies aren't enjoyable at all; after several biopsies and a lot of pain, I decided to go ahead with the surgery and have it scheduled for the near future. I knew certain aspects of my life might change forever as a result of the surgery, but I also knew it was extremely costly and totally life disrupting to continue on with the routine scheduled biopsies. I was a young man and assumed I still had a long life ahead of me.

Throughout that time, there were several postponements of the court case due to my health situation. Additionally, both my parents had reached a stage with their own health situation where remaining in their home was not an option. Living in the small town they did, there wasn't an adequately equipped facility to care for them. After lengthy and at times grueling discussions with my siblings, I was eventually able to bring my parents to Oklahoma City so I could be close and assist in their care the remainder of their lives.

My dad was the first one to arrive in Oklahoma City. He'd just received a knee replacement back home and wasn't doing well in his recovery or in subsequent physical therapy. The initial facility he was in just wasn't working out. After his arrival in Oklahoma City, there was a marked improvement with his progress. He fit right in with everyone at the new facility and the move appeared to be the right one.

In the meantime, my mom had fallen and broken her hip. I immediately had her transferred by ambulance to Oklahoma City for the surgery. Ironically, it was with the assistance of a good friend, previously employed by my former employer where all my legal battles originated from, that I was able to obtain the services of one of the best orthopedic surgeons in Oklahoma City to perform my mom's hip surgery. Everything went well and after initial therapy in a rehabilitation hospital, I was able to transfer her to the same facility my dad was in.

It'd end up I'd eventually run into several professionals long gone from that former employer, many of them having experienced some of the same problems I experienced when I was in their employment. Some of us eventually began to stay in touch on a regular basis.

With everything going on at that point in my life, I turned to God many times and asked for his strength and guidance. There was a tremendous amount of care needed for my parents and I had to determine the best way to go about everything; my significant other thought of my parents as his own and he was a life saver in assisting with their care. I needed to make some decisions, I needed to free up more of my time for my parents and my own health as well, in addition to working as many hours as I possibly could at my job.

What that meant was ending the ordeal with the court case; it'd been going on so very long with no progress made due to all the continuances and postponements. I knew I'd prevail and win in the end when it came for my day in court, but would I be around to have that day. After some lengthy discussions with my attorney, a plea agreement was worked out. It actually wasn't in my best interest in that I'd never get my day in court with all the true facts and circumstances eventually revealed and proven on my behalf. However, it was in the best interest of my health, the health of my parents, and the well being of my sons and significant other. It also freed up more time than I originally imagined, time I desperately needed; the court ordeal was finally over.

Throughout all the ordeals and legal battles resulting from my former employment, I realized being a minority was definitely more of a strike against me than I could've ever known. I'm not saying an exact homosexual count would be definitive in rendering a minority designation, as I'd be extremely curious to see the results if a gadget existed that could be scanned across the forehead of every individual and determine with accuracy whether that individual was a homosexual or heterosexual; the count could easily be closer than one thinks. There're sure to be millions of individuals in the entire world who are homosexuals; for reasons of family, safety, persecution, legalities, governments, employment, and a host of other reasons many are totally closeted possibly never coming out. Regardless, a case definitely exists currently for minority status of homosexuals as that exact count could never be possible; until an exact count could be possible and ultimately performed resulting in unequivocal equality existing among homosexuals and heterosexuals, that minority status is warranted. The word gay carries such a damaging stigma in so many circles of society.

One doesn't choose to be gay; one chooses to live a lie or live the truth. What would God want us to do?

12

Proceeding Ahead With Surgery And Family

The nursing facility in Oklahoma City my parents were in was extremely close to my office. I'd go by to check on them in the mornings on my way to the office and in the evenings on my way home. Some days I'd totally surprise them and stop by at lunch as well. At that time, my significant other's employment was fairly close and he too would stop by in the mornings on his way to work. Many times he and dad would go outside to smoke a cigarette together. The weekend was an especially fun time for my parents as we'd be able to stay longer and many times would either eat something with them or take soft serve ice cream to them; it was truly an enjoyable time for everyone, we even became close friends with many of the staff and other residents.

After a period of time, I felt they'd become somewhat

settled in; my siblings would come periodically to visit and that'd give me and my significant other some relief. My mom was recovering from her hip surgery and things appeared headed in the direction where I could schedule my own prostate surgery. Just as I was reviewing dates for my surgery, mom fell again and broke her other hip. My stamina was questionable at that time so I asked my siblings for some help; my brother was the one to come to my rescue, he was always available no matter the situation.

I stayed at mom's side from the moment I arrived after her fall up to the time she was taken to the surgery room. My brother and I waited in the hospital family room during the surgery and hours appeared to have gone by. Finally after several hours, the doctor came out and told us everything went well. We both eventually went home to get some rest as mom was fairly sedated; we knew the next day would be another long tiring one. My brother decided to stay a few days to help sit with mom. She needed someone there constantly the first several days as she was bound and determined to get out of bed; her dementia had worsened.

Life continued on and I decided to wait a little longer before I scheduled my own surgery; I wanted to be certain mom and dad could get along without me for a few weeks during my own recovery. I knew my significant other could handle the care of my parents, but I felt more comfortable waiting.

During that time, my dad was going through a period

of depression and saw no reason to live any longer; he was always closest to my sister back home and after a few visits from her, he somewhat perked up. Mom's dementia was continuing to worsen; the thought finally entered my mind I could be waiting a very long time for my own surgery so I decided to ask my siblings to come down at different times to assist with mom and dad and I'd go ahead with my surgery.

I telephoned my urologist's office and his nurse scheduled the surgery. The scheduled date appeared at the time to work with everyone's schedule, everyone except my youngest son's schedule. He was still living in Los Angeles and was working in production for a television series being filmed at the time; I told him I'd be fine. I didn't want him to schedule time off and miss any of the filming. He was adamant on being at the hospital during the surgery and nothing I'd say would change that. My brother and his wife decided they'd be more help to me in all areas if they came right after the surgery; that proved to be a great choice. My sisters, rather than coming at different times to spread out the assistance with the care of mom and dad, decided they wanted to come together at the same time; that proved not to be such a good choice as too much company for my mom at the same time would always worsen her dementia. Everyone else lived in the area so scheduling wasn't an issue.

I was extremely nervous before the surgery and knew it could change my life in many ways forever. The day arrived and the time came to be prepped for the surgery; my significant other and my youngest son waited in the hospital family room during the procedure. Before I knew it, I was in a hospital bed barely cognizant of my surroundings. My significant other told me the doctor talked with him mentioning it appeared everything went well and he'd be by later to check on me. He also told me my son had a plane to catch and he needed to get him to the airport. They both gave me a kiss on the check and I evidently fell asleep; the next thing I remembered was my oldest son waking me up asking how I was doing. Before long my significant other was back from the airport and mentioned he'd stopped by the nursing facility on his way back to assure my parents I was doing fine; he said he didn't see my sisters as they were at their hotel resting up from the trip down. In a short time I was sleeping again.

I really didn't come totally around until early the next morning; I remember being very hungry and hurting like hell. The first thing I noticed was a bouquet of balloons on the night stand, my sons and ex-wife sent them; behind the balloons was a large plant sent by my employer. I received a few telephone calls that day and before long it was evening with a couple visitors showing up.

I was released on the third day and my oldest son came over to sit with me part of the day until my significant other came home from work. I was pretty much confined to bed rest for a few days with a follow up appointment a few days later. My brother had already telephoned to check on my condition and told me he and his wife would be down in a few days after my sisters left; I had yet to see or hear a word from either of my sisters who were already in Oklahoma City.

I was experiencing an extreme amount of pain the first few days and it continued on. I telephoned my doctor's office early one morning and his nurse called in a prescription for pain medication immediately. I couldn't get in touch with anyone to pick it up for me and my significant other wouldn't be home from work until around six that evening. I decided to telephone my dad at the nursing facility to have him ask one of my sisters if they'd go pick it up and bring it to me; he told me they'd left for breakfast and he'd ask them when they returned. My sister's husband eventually called me back saying he'd checked with my sisters and he just couldn't do it; he told me they thought he'd probably get lost. I couldn't believe what I was hearing. They'd all been to the store where my pharmacy was several times during their visits to see mom and dad; it was right down the street from my office one way and the other way just down the street from the nursing facility. They'd also been by the house with my brother on one of their previous visits and my other sister had been by the house on two occasions prior to that; it was a little less than a twenty minute drive with only three major turns from the nursing facility to the house and I told my brother in law I'd talk them through the entire drive over the cell phone if necessary. I really didn't fault my brother in law because I knew again he was only relaying the thoughts of my sisters.

Dad called me back a little later after my sisters and brother in law left to go shopping; he again apologized for his daughter, my dear sister. He said, "J.C., you know how your sister can be, please don't be upset with me, if I could get out and drive I'd go get it myself." I told dad not to worry and I'd try someone else. I never did find anyone else and after a day of excruciating pain, finally got some relief when my significant other arrived home later in the day; we ended up in the emergency room.

We arrived home late that evening after receiving a shot for pain relief in the emergency room. My significant other wanted to go give my sisters and brother in law a piece of his mind for not wanting to get my pain medication earlier in the day; he told me he saw the hurt in my eyes, not just from the physical pain, but from their actions as well. He was right I'd never in my entire life witnessed such hatred exhibited by family members under such circumstances, both at that time and previously as well. It was difficult for me to totally comprehend how someone could be so cruel in their behavior no matter what their reasoning or justification was. It was also hard to believe such actions resulted totally from their homophobia; a part of me wondered what role selfishness may have played. It had always been known by everyone in the family how my sisters could be, it was just something everyone chose to overlook; it was easier to get along that way.

PROCEEDING AHEAD WITH SURGERY AND FAMILY

I honestly prayed to God for forgiveness of my sisters' actions; I was so deeply hurt emotionally, it was my only way of going forward and finding the faith and courage to forgive them myself.

I really missed seeing mom and dad while I was recovering; my significant other still went by to check on them throughout that time and took them whatever they needed. My sisters finally went home and my brother and his wife arrived from Virginia to help out. I never did see or hear anything from my sisters the entire time they were in Oklahoma City, other than that telephone call from my brother in law. My brother and his wife came over to the house to visit and check on me the day they arrived. They stayed in Oklahoma City a few days to help with mom and dad and before they flew back to Virginia stopped by again to say goodbye.

It was time for my first follow up appointment with my urologist. I was told the cancer was confined to the prostate and it looked as though he got it all. I was totally relieved to hear that news. He went on to tell me I'd have to keep the catheter in for several more days and could experience some incontinence for an unknown period of time after its removal. I was also told I could experience erectile dysfunction for an unknown period of time once the healing process was complete.

The following day I had my significant other drive me to the nursing facility to see mom and dad. I was so excited to see them I thought I was going to pee my pants, thank God I still had the catheter in. It was so good to see them; everyone got teary eyed. I told my dad I might have to borrow some of his adult diapers when I got the catheter out and he got a big kick out of that. Even though my mom's dementia was definitely elevated, she always knew who I was and the first thing she said to me was, "J.C., go out to the kitchen and have some cookies I baked for you; I was worried about you, why are you so late getting home from work?" She went on to say, "Supper will be ready soon." My mom had always been able to cook and bake just about anything. With her dementia, she thought I was still living at home and just late from work. She obviously thought she'd also baked me some cookies that afternoon. I left her room for a moment pretending to go in the kitchen to eat some cookies. When I got back she asked me if they were as good as usual; of course I said, "Better."

Before my significant other and I left the nursing facility, we wheeled mom and dad over to the piano in the family area and mom played for us. She was quite the pianist her entire life and only got better with age. Other residents of the nursing facility wheeled themselves over and everyone was royally entertained. It was very difficult leaving after our visit; not only did it pick my parents up, but it picked me up more than they'd ever know.

FAMILY ENTERTAINMENT PROVIDED BY MY MOTHER
AT THE NURSING FACILITY

LIVING THE DIFFERENCE

I was really getting bored throughout that entire period of recovery even though my oldest son came out often to visit and my youngest in California called several times. I was still experiencing a few minor complications from the surgery and my urologist suggested I remain at home a while longer. It was at that time I decided to do an outline of my life experiences that I'd eventually write a book about. I'd always wanted to contribute to society my experiences and whatever knowledge they might bestow on someone possibly seeking guidance through a difficult period of time in their own life, as well as mutually benefiting others in the process.

Before I knew it, I received a telephone call from my urologist's office informing me the last blood workup came back with great results; I could go back to the office half days a few weeks and then try full days after that. Since my surgery was a radical perineal prostatectomy, it was extremely painful to sit for extended periods of time; however, I was glad to be going back to work. I was also told I could remove the catheter myself and be prepared for a runaway garden hose; it wasn't only a runaway, but appeared the turn off valve was stuck. I was forced to wear adult diapers for a period of time.

My first day back at the office was a long one, even though I only stayed half a day. It was good to see everyone and nice to have felt missed. It was extremely uncomfortable sitting in my chair, there was an inflatable cushion on the seat and I was wearing an adult diaper; I felt like I was in one of those padded Sumo wrestler suits. I forgot to take extra diapers with me as it'd been some time since I'd packed a diaper bag; I needed a change so I rigged up a makeshift diaper with scotch tape and paper towels. To this day, the office manager is still probably wondering were all the paper towels disappeared to that day!

Eventually I went to work full days and appeared I was back in the saddle again, at least at the office. I was still experiencing the incontinency and could only hope the erectile dysfunction would possibly resolve itself with ample time, healing, and/or medication. A huge concern at that time was the high level of anxiety I was experiencing subsequent to the surgery and nothing I'd do seemed to help the situation; I was sure the lingering side effects had a lot to do with it. My urologist suggested attending a support group of males having been through similar surgery; eventually I found one on line and chatted in the group room a few times.

I met an individual on line who was somewhat in the same situation I was in; however, his surgery was several months prior to mine and he was still experiencing many of the same side effects. One difference in our situations being sexual preferences, he was a heterosexual. We met for lunch one day and ended up talking a couple hours. His main concern was the incontinency he was experiencing after such a long time, as he still wasn't able to control his bladder. He told me every time his bladder even began to feel partially full, it'd drain itself without any warning and he couldn't control it. He wasn't as concerned over the erectile dysfunction; he was just so relieved his cancer was gone and mentioned he and his wife enjoyed intimacy in other ways. It appeared his anxiety level was substantially lower than mine, partially from the prolonged passage of time subsequent to his surgery. He finally asked me if being a homosexual might have something to do with my high level of anxiety due to the erectile dysfunction issue, I asked him to elaborate. He was a little embarrassed, but said, "Isn't that bodily function extremely important in the gay world?" My response was, "Isn't that bodily function extremely important in the straight world?" I knew what he meant, but was still somewhat irritated with such a shallow question.

While I was still wearing a diaper at that time, my bladder control was definitely better than his and improving; I felt I'd have total control in the very near future. One of my main concerns, in addition to my high level of anxiety, was whether I'd overcome the erectile dysfunction. I was in a catch twenty two situation in that I definitely needed the medication I was on for anxiety and depression, but that medication weighed heavily on my erectile dysfunction. The stress I was under with the increasingly demanding task of caring for my parents, much of that stress due to the constant turmoil that existed in dealing with my sisters over certain topics of care, didn't help the situation.

Time went on and the anxiety and depression worsened, I finally realized there was a direct correlation to the deteriorating situation with my sisters. It appeared the reasoning for such mentally abusive behavior did result from their homophobia. One evening while on the telephone with my youngest sister differences were voiced as to the best solution for a care issue relating to dad, all of a sudden the conversation turned ugly with her saying, "It's no wonder I feel this way, you're just a frickin' *faggot*, do you realize how embarrassed mom and dad are of you?" I responded with a few choice words of my own, but I don't think she heard them all as the telephone was slammed down as I was responding. I didn't think for a moment my parents were embarrassed of me, maybe a little disappointed I was born a homosexual, but not embarrassed; she only wanted me to think that.

In a couple weeks the holiday season was upon us. Mom's dementia was to the point she had to be transferred to a hospital with a special short term geriatric wing for patients with dementia and other psychological disorders; how long she'd be there we didn't know. Dad was staying in bed most the time and was getting some serious bed sores; every day when I'd stop by the nursing facility to check on him, I'd make sure he was up in his wheel chair, but by lunch time he'd be back in bed.

Dad telephoned me at my office Christmas Eve day to tell me my sisters surprised him and were down for a visit, he wanted me and my significant other to stop by later in the evening to have Christmas Eve dinner with everyone; my brother and his family weren't able to be there.

As reluctant as we were due to my sisters being there, we didn't want to disappoint dad. We took gifts for everyone, thought the gesture might render the evening a bit more enjoyable. We handed them out when we arrived and wished everyone a Merry Christmas; all we heard back were minor utterances, of course dad was excited and gave us hugs and kisses.

We were all sitting in the family visiting room with conversation abound except with us, it was as if we weren't in the room at all; dad and my sister's youngest daughter were the only ones responding to our conversation. My sisters got up and walked out of the room, my significant other followed them. In a few minutes he came back and whispered to me he needed to talk with me in private. I told dad we had to go check with the nurse on something and would be back in a moment. He told me he tried to talk with my sisters asking them if they knew how much their abusive behavior toward us hurt me; he went on to say he even mentioned to them it not only affected the two of us, but their own mom and dad as well. My oldest sister slapped him in the face and walked away.

When we tried to get back in the family visiting room, my sisters had already returned and locked the door from the inside so we couldn't get in. I was furious so I went to the charge nurse and told her what was going on. She immediately opened the door with her master key and made my sisters and their families leave the premises. I felt terribly sorry for my dad; he knew how they were, but couldn't do a thing. Later, he telephoned them at their hotel room and told them to come back immediately to apologize for their behavior. When they arrived, it was the same thing all over again so I told dad it was ok; I told him we'd leave and come back later after they left. On our way out the door, my oldest sister came up behind me and slapped me up the side of my head. What is it about slapping someone up the side of the head, why do certain individuals get off doing that? She went on to say, "You belong in the *loony bin* with mom."

Little did she know that was exactly where we were headed; we were excited to be going to the *loony bin*, people there were actually saner than she was. We arrived in time to sit down with mom and visit while she ate Christmas Eve dinner. She was so excited to see us she wouldn't finish eating because she couldn't wait to get to the piano and play us some Christmas songs. We gave mom her gifts and after a nice visit went on our way to deliver gifts to other family members and friends.

Throughout that time, with all the legal and medical expenses I'd incurred over the previous few years, I was forced to file bankruptcy. I filed chapter thirteen as I personally felt obligated to repay as much of my debt as I could within my means. Of course my sisters thought it was terribly irresponsible of me to file bankruptcy; they found out in conversations with my brother. At that point, it really didn't matter what they thought.

13

Life's Journey Saddens

The starting of a new year was upon me. I was determined to make the most of it; I went forward with total conviction everything happened for a reason and I'd become a better person from those experiences gained from my past. I couldn't change who or what I was, but at least was somewhat more informed on the general public's perception, acceptance, and behavior toward homosexuals, including the behavior of certain members of my own family. I also gained a totally new and different perspective on the value of life; it's extremely valuable, only God knows what tomorrow will bring, every one of us should accept and live each day as if it were our last or our first, whichever way you choose to see it.

I knew the possibility existed my parents wouldn't be around much longer; I wanted to make their time left as enjoyable as I possibly could. I decided it better I wasn't around whenever my sisters would come for a visit, it was too hard for mom and dad to witness the obvious hatred my sisters exhibited toward me and my significant other; mom and dad loved us all dearly, they didn't need to be put in that situation.

Time went on and a ghost from the past surfaced. I never told anyone at the time, but somehow the fact of my working on a book detailing certain experiences in my life appeared to become known to the employer from hell that caused my previous legal hassles. I received a telephone call one morning at the office from an anonymous caller informing me if any reference to that employer was made in my book detailing any of the facts or circumstances of the ordeal, I wouldn't be around long to reap any benefit from the published work. Before I could respond the telephone was slammed down. There weren't any caller ID capabilities on my office telephone and I didn't feel comfortable getting my current employer involved in any attempt to identify the caller in other ways through the telephone company or from their own telephone records.

I didn't know what to do or if I should even attempt doing anything. I'd been through enough relating to that entire ordeal and decided it was possibly nothing more than an idle threat that in all likelihood would never materialize. I even gave thought the threat could've come from someone else with extreme hatred toward me; not that I thought many people did, I could only think of two other individuals. However, I still went through a period of time reviewing in my mind anyone having knowledge of the ordeal, as well as knowledge of my book intentions and it just wasn't worth consideration of even confronting anyone at that point.

In the meantime, my mom was to be released from the hospital's short term geriatric wing for return back to the nursing facility; however, the nursing facility wouldn't take her back due to her elevated dementia. I immediately began searching for a facility that could care for mom on a long term basis with her dementia; it was quite a chore to find one. I finally got her in a facility with a separate section for those individuals with varying levels of dementia. It was quite a distance from both my dad's facility and my office; I'd just have to split my time between the two of them.

I had to cut down the number of daily visits to my parents. I made a loop; I'd leave real early in the mornings to go see mom on my way to the office and I adjusted my lunch schedule leaving early in the afternoon to go see dad on my way home from the office. During that time, my significant other began a new job in the opposite direction and his visits were limited to the weekends.

We decided to begin a search for a house in the city and move off our acreage. It was the only way we'd be able to fit everything in our busy schedules and still manage to find a little time for ourselves; the savings in commute time, as well as less time required for property maintenance would make that possible. It'd be some time before we'd put the property up for sale though as certain projects needed to be completed to realize the full value of the property.

One evening when I arrived home from visiting dad, I picked up the mail from the mailbox on my way down the drive and there was a large manila envelope in the box with no address, return address, or postage; obviously someone placed it there. I opened it to find an article cut out from some publication, the way it was cut left no indication as to the source; the article dealt with homosexuality being the work of the devil and those practicing such sexual practices were sure to go to hell. It didn't look like newspaper or magazine print, but rather a part of some locally produced pamphlet. There was no reference cited for support of the contents of the article; it appeared to be merely an individual opinion put to print. I thought it rather strange to receive it so close to that telephone call I'd received earlier.

Receiving the article the way I did at least allowed me to pretty much cross two previously suspected individuals off my list, it would've been virtually impossible for them to have left it; not that I was ready to pursue the source of either of the incidents. I threw the manila envelope and the article in the outdoor trash dumpster before my significant other arrived home that evening; I buried them at the very bottom.

A part of me was a little scared, living as far out in the

country as we did with someone obviously knowing our sexual preferences, as well as where we lived, put me on edge; I was thankful we had an electronic security gate. I still decided not to worry my significant other as those incidents appeared directed toward me. Maybe the article came from some redneck Oklahoma family living in the area just voicing their own opinion with no harm intended.

The health of my parents continued to worsen and I received a telephone call late one evening informing me my mom should probably go to the hospital, they didn't think it was an emergency, just a precaution. I rushed over and she wasn't very coherent so I immediately took her to the hospital emergency room. They did some blood work and performed a few other tests, the doctor eventually determined she'd suffered a mild heart attack; he admitted her to the hospital. She finally came around and knew exactly who I was. She wanted me to sit next to her bed and hold her hand; she was so sweet and precious, I stayed awake at her side the entire night holding her hand.

The next morning her doctor scheduled a heart catheterization procedure for later in the week; he wanted her to get some of her strength back before the procedure. She was resting comfortably that morning so I went home, showered, and went on to work. That evening I went by to check on dad and he was very confused so I made the decision not to tell him about mom's heart attack. He was talking about his own parents, along with his brothers and sisters, the majority of them long passed many years prior. He really didn't know what was going on and doubts existed in my mind he actually knew who I was.

I received a telephone call around eleven the next morning, my dad was non responsive and in an ambulance on his way to the emergency room; I ran out the office door and drove like a maniac to the hospital. I arrived just as the ambulance was unloading my dad, his eyes were open, but his face was already turning blue; I held his hand on the way to the emergency room until they made me step aside and wait outside the room. After several minutes the doctor came out and told me my dad had passed away. I couldn't believe my very special dad was gone; I knew he was in a better place, but I wanted more time to spend with him.

I wasn't able to make any telephone calls right away as I couldn't stop crying. The hospital chaplain took me to a special room and we prayed together. I finally made the necessary telephone calls and was then allowed in the room to sit with dad until the funeral home arrived; my significant other arrived by that time and we both sat with dad holding his hands. I'd lost one of the best dads anyone could ever hope to have.

After the funeral home took his body, we went to the other hospital across town where mom was. We didn't tell her about dad as she'd already been through enough; we stayed for some time and then left to go home. On our way to the parking garage my oldest son telephoned and wanted me to go with him to see his grandpa that evening, he hadn't heard the news yet. When I told him he was very sad, he'd just lost his last grandpa and he'd planned on visiting him that evening; he went ahead and met us at the parking garage and the three of us went to dinner.

The funeral would be a few days off to give other family members travel time to get home; it'd be held in my home town of Guymon, Oklahoma. My youngest son flew in from Los Angeles the day before; other family members arrived at various times. My dad was very well liked and there was a large turnout to celebrate his life. I gave the eulogy at the service, but was unable to finish due to emotions. There was an informal family gathering at my sister's house after the service; however, my immediate family felt unwelcome. Certain family members (my sisters), along with others from their own families totally ignored my significant other and me the entire day and wouldn't even respond to our initiated conversation. It was just as well because we needed to get back to Oklahoma City to check on mom; she'd just had the catheterization procedure performed a couple days prior to dad's funeral and was still in the hospital. Of course my brother and his family made every individual feel welcome that day, including me and my significant other.

We arrived back in Oklahoma City and immediately went to the hospital to check on mom. She was doing fine except her dementia had worsened; however, she was still to be dismissed in a couple days. In the meantime,

I'd received a telephone call from her nursing facility the morning of my dad's funeral informing me they wouldn't allow her back due to her combined dementia and frail health. I found out nursing facilities were extremely selective and wanted residents in fairly decent health; residents having left the facility to go to the hospital, depending on their prognosis, many times weren't allowed to return. That made for a much easier case load for their staff by basically getting rid of residents returning from the hospital with worsening conditions.

I took a couple extra days off from the office to search and check on facilities suitable for mom. I really didn't know where to start so I got out the yellow pages and started calling around. I ended up visiting over a half dozen different facilities and finally located one I felt would be good for mom; they assured me they weren't as selective as far as worsening conditions and the resident's ability to remain with the facility.

I moved her belongings to the new facility the next morning and went to pick her up from the hospital that afternoon. She was hilarious on our way to the new place; she was totally confused as to where I was taking her, but made sure along the entire route I stopped at all yellow lights, not red, and that I not go over twenty miles per hour. At one point she turned to me and pointed her finger at me saying, "J.C., I know you're speeding!"

I finally returned to work and thanked everyone for the beautiful plant they'd sent to my dad's funeral, along with the wonderful cards I'd received from many of them. I was hoping for some smooth sailing for a period of time as I was totally exhausted and drained of energy. I even went to my family doctor that first afternoon back to get a prescription for a sedative so I could sleep nights; I hadn't been able to sleep nights for quite a few days and was definitely feeling it.

I caught myself many times those first few days back automatically heading toward dad's nursing facility; I really missed seeing and taking a cup of coffee to him as I walked in his room. We became extremely close during the time I cared for him; we'd always been close, but something was different, we'd become buddies. I really felt lost without him.

During that time, whenever any spare time surfaced I'd work on the remaining projects on our acreage; we still wanted to sell and move to the city. I probably shouldn't have done as much physical labor as I did because many of my remaining problem areas from my own surgery weren't improving and at times I felt they'd worsened. I needed to slow down, but had a difficult time getting that accomplished; every time I thought I could something else would come up.

One evening on my way home from the office, a feeling came over me I was being followed. There was a man in a red truck appearing to be going my way; every time I turned or changed lanes, he'd do the same. I decided to go around a lake road and come upon my property from the opposite direction, he followed. I realized at that point I was definitely being followed and decided not to pull in the property. About a mile from the property, the driver forced me off the road; he quickly backed up, rolled the passenger window down and yelled, "Drop it!"

I was trembling when I got home. My significant other was working late that evening so I was home alone. I couldn't figure out what the driver meant, I'd dropped the civil law suit against my former employer a long time before that; being so close to those other two previous incidents, I assumed it had to be related to the book I was working on. I decided right then I'd not discuss my work on the book with anyone other than my significant other, I even decided to prolong the work on it and wait on publication submission until a ways down the road. I thought if talk or gossip about the book ceased, they'd assume I'd given the project up. Whether or not it was my former employer, it didn't matter; someone obviously didn't want me to write the book. I didn't have much spare time to devote to it anyway.

Around that time I went for another check up with my urologist. I was told I definitely needed to slow down. While I was in his office he decided to try an injection procedure to determine if it'd help with my erectile dysfunction; I was given a shot at the base of my penis. Within minutes a part of my body was at full attention and wouldn't stand down; he told me that was good and showed my equipment to be in working order. However, after thirty minutes of being at attention, it hurt like hell. He reversed the procedure, within a couple minutes everything was back to normal and I went home. I decided I'd wait for my erectile dysfunction to get better with time. I was quite embarrassed during that procedure, the entire time his nurse was in the room and assisted at his side.

Meanwhile, my mom appeared to be getting along great in the new facility. One day when I was visiting she asked me where dad was. I decided she needed to know so I told her dad had passed away while she was in the hospital recovering from her heart attack. While her dementia was definitely present, she was as sharp as a tack when you least expected it; her response was, "I thought he'd probably died because I hadn't heard from him in a long time."

Time went on and things finally settled down somewhat. My significant other and I found some spare time and finished the majority of our unfinished projects on our acreage. We were getting close to putting it up for sale. We'd always sold our own properties without realtors and would do the same with the acreage. I started gathering information on all the improvements to the property so I could do my own analysis of original versus replacement costs on the entire acreage, including the dwelling and all outdoor structures; I needed a starting point in coming up with a value for the property.

Mom's dementia eventually worsened to the point her current facility at the time informed me she needed to be transferred to the same short term geriatric wing of the hospital she'd been in before; they went on to inform me they wouldn't be able to care for her upon release from the hospital. I went back and forth with them on the assurance they gave me earlier that their facility could accommodate a resident with worsening conditions, including dementia. They finally agreed to take her back, but I'd have to pay them extra to reserve her room. That didn't sit well with me because that facility had ample spare rooms at the time. I decided to cancel her room because it appeared it was a total imposition on them to properly care for my mom. I immediately went to pick mom up and took her to the hospital.

She ended up staying several weeks in the hospital; not only did her dementia take a drastic turn for the worse, but other areas of her health continued to deteriorate. She continued to recognize me and my significant other, even our voices. One Saturday afternoon we went to visit and took her some ice cream, she was in the middle of receiving a bath. We stood outside her room visiting with the staff and other patients and all of a sudden heard mom yell, "J.C., is that you, don't leave, I'll be right out." She heard us talking. The attendant giving her bath told us mom wouldn't even let her finish, she wanted to get right out to see us.

In the meantime, I'd arranged her fourth nursing facility; it'd be her last. A few days prior to her release from the hospital, my significant other and I painted her room at the new facility, put up some new curtains, moved in some new furniture, and put a brand new comforter on her bed that matched the new curtains. The day of her release from the hospital, I drove her to the new facility and stayed the morning with her to help get her settled in. Before I left later in the day to go to work, she sang and played me a song on the piano. The words were so personal and special I said, "Mom, I've never heard that song before." Her response was, "I made it up just for you." I started to cry and gave her a big bear hug. That day was Friday.

When we went to visit her on Saturday, she wasn't quite as coherent; the nurses told us she was up all night looking for dad. We stayed with her until she went to sleep for a nap. The next day we got there a little before noon, she was real tired again, we stayed until she went to sleep; before she drifted off she gave us both a big kiss and told us she loved us. Later that afternoon at the house, I told my significant other something didn't seem right and I was going to see mom; before I could even leave the house, the nursing facility called and told me she was on her way to the emergency room, she was non responsive.

My significant other and I rushed to the hospital and she was already in one of the emergency examining rooms with the doctor. We waited several minutes; finally the doctor came out telling us he'd revived her and wanted to know if we wanted her on a ventilator. Mom's wish was to be on one unless it was determined she'd never come off it or had brain damage. I immediately telephoned everyone and my brother flew right out. Between me, my significant other, and my brother, someone was with mom around the clock holding her hand.

After a brain scan, it was determined while being revived, she'd suffered brain damage due to lack of oxygen to the brain. The ventilator was turned off. Mom hung on without the ventilator for a couple days and finally passed on to be with dad. That moment was one of the darkest moments in my life. My mom and I had a bond no one could come close to; I'd lost the person who gave me birth, the best person and mom I'd ever known.

Her funeral would be in a couple days when all family members could be there. The behavior of my sisters hadn't changed, not a word was said to me or my significant other, the one who provided more care to their own parents than they did the last few years; I couldn't have made it through that time had it not been for him. My oldest son was very distraught with the behavior of my sisters and after the services jogged out to the cemetery to clear his mind.

I went through an extremely difficult period of time in my life shortly thereafter; I even questioned my own faith. What God would let so many trails and tribulations occur in one's life over such a short period of time? I was numb.

IN LOVING MEMORY OF MY MOTHER AND FATHER

14

Finding The Light Again
And Continuing On

Was I being punished for being a homosexual? Some wanted me to think so; after some time, I began to wonder myself. I was having a difficult time coping with life. I even had a difficult time talking with God; I went through the motions each and every day, but that was it.

Something needed to give I needed a definite purpose in my life. I stayed home from the office one day trying to find the faith I so desperately needed in order to continue on. I prayed to God for guidance; I spent the entire day alone with him. After several hours, I recognized and regained a good portion of the faith I knew was somewhere within me.

I thanked God for the privilege of having known such wonderful parents, as well as the privilege of having so many loving individuals in my life, especially my sons, my significant other, and my brother. I knew without a doubt God loved me and wanted me to live a truthful life, the life I was born to live. I also knew at that time, a part of my purpose in life was to help and enlighten others.

TRUSTING MY FAITH IN GOD

I immediately moved forward with progress on my book again. At that time, more than ever before, I wanted a vehicle available for individuals to use in navigating through some of the troubling times of identifying and dealing with their own personal feelings, as well as their own true identity; I also wanted a vehicle available as soon as possible for others to learn the importance of understanding and accepting those individuals. By that time, I knew without a doubt the knowledge to be gained from my own experiences and insight into so many diverse situations would be that ultimate vehicle.

I didn't care there were individuals out there dead set against my book; it'd be bigger than them. It'd be something no one would be able to stop. It'd be something everyone would need to read. I knew there could easily be damaging repercussions from having my book published, but I was more than willing to take that chance. God was good to me; my book would be my way of giving back!

Eventually, my significant other and I finished every project on our acreage and put it on the market. We put signs outside the entrance gate and along major roads directing potential buyers to the property. We began with an open house, producing a significant amount of foot traffic. In a few weeks we had several interested parties and ended up with a contract on the property. The first contract fell through with another contract replacing it shortly thereafter.

There was one couple early on who just couldn't get

past the fact we were a gay couple living in a house together; they even went so far as inquiring who slept where. They came back a couple times voicing a definite interest in the property. Every time, the husband would bring up some question dealing with our sexual preferences. Either he was closeted or just overly homophobic. We finally told them we thought the property contained too many *h-o-m-o-s-e-x-u-a-l* features for them; we never heard back from either of them again. By the way, I actually didn't think such features existed, but evidently they did!

During that time, we'd contracted with a builder to build us a home in town. It'd be smaller than our home in the country, but that was ok with us; we wanted to downsize since all the kids were grown. We changed many of the existing features of the floor plans as we wanted a more custom look; doing so prolonged the completion somewhat.

It finally came time for closing on the sale of the acreage and we were forced to live in a hotel for a couple weeks. Not only was the completion of our new home delayed from all the custom work, but several days of torrential rains made pouring the driveway impossible; you can't get an occupancy permit without a driveway. We finally closed on the home and checked out of the hotel. It took some time to become accustomed to a smaller home, but we managed to adjust.

By that time my oldest son, having graduated from college, began his career in banking and my youngest son moved back to Oklahoma City to enroll in broadcasting school. Around that time, my significant other's son graduated from high school and enrolled in some college courses. We still worked at our same old boring jobs. I even gave thought to getting back into my own profession; however, I was somewhat reluctant due to the continued anxiety I'd been experiencing for several years.

My position at that time was totally lackluster with no stress involved, other than having to put up with certain employees. You'd think a company with an owner having their own gay child would be totally free of homophobia, think again! The owner was actually ok with my homosexuality. It was even one of the topics of conversation brought up by the owner in a meeting between the two of us; everything turned out great. The owner met my significant other on several different occasions and the two of them became friends.

None the less, there were many employees in the company so homophobic it created an unhealthy work environment for me. I was exposed to conversations slamming gays, with negative comments even made about the owner's own gay child. The contents of many of those conversations definitely showed the mentality of certain employees. Even though I worked closely with many of them, obviously certain ones didn't realize I was gay; if they had, many of those comments probably wouldn't have been made in front of me.

There were definitely some employees who obviously

understood homosexuality being just a mere descriptive term, like heterosexuality, and it didn't influence their behavior at all. However, there was one specific individual who was extremely difficult to be around and work with; I honestly believed it was a form of jealousy, rather than discrimination due to my sexual preferences. Either way, that employee continually harassed me at the office, while doing no wrong in the eyes of the owner. Something wasn't right; it appeared just maybe the employee knew too many secrets or confidential information about the company needing to remain behind closed doors. That conclusion was based entirely on the resulting behavior of the owner toward the harassing actions of that employee.

As a result, I lost a great deal of respect for the owner due to lack of action on many issues brought to light. It appeared to me as long as one considered the company their family and participated in most activities outside of work promoted by the company, it was easier to get along; however, if that wasn't the case it was another story. It was terribly difficult for me to consider the company family with the way I was continually treated by certain employees, as well as certain members of management. Another way of having it made in the shade was to be related to someone within the company, no matter how distant that relation may be. I struck out on all counts! Thank God I was good at what I did! Discrimination ran rampant in that company!

Regardless, in my opinion, it's definitely better in most

situations to remain closeted at the workplace. One never knows exactly where homophobia exists; I definitely speak from experience. However, certain professions, along with certain geographic locations, are more open to homosexuality; when society is more informed, it's generally more accepting.

Work continued on my book; I tried to devote a dedicated time each day to working on the manuscript. Many times emotions from certain memories got the best of me and I'd have to distance myself from the project for a period of time; during those times, not only did I distance myself, but I'd have to totally block out all aspects of the entire project from my mind, even conversations relating to it. Other times, I couldn't stay away from the computer because there was so much to talk about and put into words.

Originally, I wanted the book completed and available a few years earlier; I'd already passed numerous self-imposed arbitrary deadlines. However, delays usually have several reasons; another reason for the delay of my book was beyond my own control, it was an unexplainable timing delay. God really does work in mysterious ways; had it been completed earlier, you wouldn't have been enlightened with the following information I'm sure will amaze you, information some of you may already have been exposed to through the media.

Regrettably, a member of the legislature in Oklahoma appeared to enjoy delivering hate speeches. During one of the speeches various comments were made relating to gays; one might think the comments came from an uneducated and narrow-minded recluse. Personal and religious views were being advocated by an elected official; not only were the views slamming gays, but our own President of the United States as well for his support of certain gay events. The following is a summarized portion of those advocated views:

The nation will be destroyed by the homosexual agenda.

Societies embracing homosexuality won't last long.

Homosexuality is a bigger threat to the nation than terrorism.

City councils across the country are being infiltrated by gays.

Gay activists are going after young children two years of age or older teaching them a homosexual lifestyle is acceptable.

At the time I was exposed to those views, I honestly believed the residents of Oklahoma should definitely be concerned with having someone of such low caliber representing them in the state legislature; I still do today. An individual with that type of mentality could be dangerous;

that mentality could easily incite rioting. I ask each and every one of you to pray for that legislative member; pray the darkness will be lifted and replaced with God's guiding light.

In the meantime, my oldest son began searching for his first home. It reminded me of years ago when he began the search for his first car; at that time, we'd look and look with nothing real exciting coming along. He finally made an offer on a piece of property appearing to be of high structural integrity; however, definitely in need of some major updates. Throughout the process, my son proved to be an excellent negotiator; after several rounds with the listing agent, he obtained the property far under the asking price.

I did help him along with some of the renovations, but the majority he performed on his own. He's pretty darn good at it. If I had to find anything negative to say about his work, it'd only be he really takes his time with it; that's ok though, many of us do. It's always been comforting knowing his acceptance of me and my significant other existed; he never gave a second thought to both of us tagging along during the house hunt.

Meanwhile, my youngest son was doing great in broadcasting school. He was over visiting one evening and told me about a conversation that came up in the classroom between a few of the students expressing their own views. It was a political conversation regarding the President of the United States and one of the views was expressed by a gay student; my son's comments in return contained references to his gay dad, me. While he was telling me about that conversation, he didn't even realize a single reference to my being gay was made; it didn't matter to him. Again, it's always been comforting knowing my sons realized early on my homosexuality wasn't a choice; their acceptance of it truly made me proud. I can only hope that same knowledge and acceptance will become universal.

Unfortunately during that time, I was still battling anxiety and depression. Chances were good I'd be plagued with the illness the rest of my life. My doctor informed me while the illness was episodic, it was also hereditary. My mom experienced bouts with the illness her entire life, with the condition worsening once her age related dementia set in. My situation had always been episodic with a definitive pattern; the pattern of episodes causing my anxiety and depression were those circumstances occurring throughout my life leading to elevated levels of stress.

Helping others, staying extremely busy, and exercising were a few ways I was always able to handle the varying levels of stress; eventually, I found myself needing to supplement with prescription medication once that level got out of control. Hopefully, I'll be able to get back to that place where medication won't be necessary; the work on my book has definitely assisted me in making tremendous strides toward that goal. For me to contribute to a more peaceful coexistence among individuals should ultimately be enough medication for a lifetime.

LIVING THE DIFFERENCE

I've always wanted societies from every walk of life to become more knowledgeable and accepting of homosexuality. I've also wanted to assist individuals in realizing one doesn't choose to be gay; the only choice has always been either to live the truth or live a lie. God doesn't want us to live a lie he wants us to live the truth!

Now that I possess such a vehicle, I will continue working toward my dreams becoming reality. My future plans include local, national, and international travels promoting improved knowledge and acceptance of homosexuality, not only through my book, but through lectures as well. Throughout that course, homosexuality won't be the only topic on my agenda; all sources of discrimination will be discussed and occupy a place within the agenda.

The next chapter, my final one in this first book of an intended series, will be a destination for anyone desiring to be a part of the beginning of something new.

15

The Beginning Of Something New

I'll need help from every one of you in getting this done. It can be the beginning of something new and exciting for each and every one. While many of you may already be involved in one or more similar causes relating to homosexuality, discrimination, or other closely related topics, please don't think your contributions won't be missed here; I welcome any and all assistance. Together, we can educate the world one step at a time while welcoming in the many changes so desperately warranted, definitely needed, and long overdue.

The list below contains some of the ways you can contribute; there's no specific order of importance and the list is by no means all inclusive:

Contact your local gay awareness center offering assistance in areas they need help.

LIVING THE DIFFERENCE

Be aware of pending legislative issues and offer support where passage of a bill promotes equality among any minority, including homosexuals.

Offer loving support to anyone needing a friend or loved one in times of confusion or ultimate awareness as to their own sexual preferences.

On gay issues, if heterosexual and wanting to help, please try to understand and accept homosexuality first.

If heterosexual and you've never knowingly been around a homosexual, make it a point to knowingly do so; we don't bite and you might just find the conversation quite stimulating and enlightening.

If needed, go to the library or local bookstore and educate yourself about homosexuality; some homosexuals aren't even fully educated themselves on the subject.

Join various support groups for family and friends of homosexuals, there's always knowledge to be gained and it'll assist in other areas of your life as well.

Promote books and other publications that nurture awareness, knowledge, and acceptance of homosexuality; we need to wipe out ignorance on the subject matter.

THE BEGINNING OF SOMETHING NEW

I'll be needing assistance in many areas once I begin traveling for lectures and book signings; if interested, contact me for details:

JOECHUCKKNUDSON@GMAIL.COM

Think of all the possibilities, think of all the fun in helping others, and especially, think of the ultimate rewards. Homosexuals and heterosexuals alike need to join in. It's time to try a more personal approach to educating the general public on certain issues many are ignorant of or misinformed on. It's time for young individuals having difficulty with their own identity to have the proper knowledge available for guidance through those tough times; what parent wouldn't want that for their child!

Please use the next few pages to write down your own thoughts, suggestions, comments, or questions; you're sure to have many by now:

_____

_____

_____

_____

_____

_____

_____

_____

LIVING THE DIFFERENCE

THE BEGINNING OF SOMETHING NEW

_____

_____

_____

_____

_____

_____

_____

_____

_____

_____

_____

_____

_____

_____

_____

_____

_____

_____

_____

_____

_____

_____

_____

_____

_____

LIVING THE DIFFERENCE

_____

_____

_____

_____

_____

_____

_____

_____

_____

_____

_____

_____

_____

_____

_____

_____

_____

_____

_____

_____

_____

I look forward to hearing from you and possibly meeting at a lecture or book signing.

SHARING TIME WITH FRIENDS AND OTHERS

TO BE CONTINUED …

P.S. You can follow efforts and progress toward the cause, as well as updates on upcoming sequels and other writings at *www.thegaylyblogger.blogspot.com*.